Flying Lessons for Leaders and Managers

Lynn Karl Nordby

Published by BookLocker.com, Inc., Bradenton, Florida.

Printed on acid-free paper.

BookLocker.com, Inc.
2016

First Edition

DISCLAIMER

This book details the author's personal experiences with and opinions about leadership and management.

The author and publisher are providing this book and its contents on an "as is" basis and make no representations or warranties of any kind with respect to this book or its contents. The author and publisher disclaim all such representations and warranties. In addition, the author and publisher do not represent or warrant that the information accessible via this book is accurate, complete or current.

The statements made about products and services have not been evaluated by the U.S. government. Please consult with your own legal or accounting professional regarding the suggestions and recommendations made in this book.

Except as specifically stated in this book, neither the author or publisher, nor any authors, contributors, or other representatives will be liable for damages arising out of or in connection with the use of this book. This is a comprehensive limitation of liability that applies to all damages of any kind, including (without limitation) compensatory; direct, indirect or consequential damages; loss of data, income or profit; loss of or damage to property and claims of third parties.

Lynn Nordby

You understand that this book is not intended as a substitute for consultation with a licensed legal or accounting professional.

This book provides content related to leadership and management topics. As such, use of this book implies your acceptance of this disclaimer.

Table of Contents

Introduction

My father, Clifford Nordby, was a city manager, serving in Alaska, California, Oregon and Montana. I didn't set out to follow in his footsteps but here I am anyway. He didn't become a city manager until later in his work life and he loved it. He often told me how he wished he'd discovered the profession sooner. This book is dedicated to him.

After a career in public management I had the opportunity to work for MRSC, the Municipal Research and Services Center of Washington, a not for profit organization that benefitted me throughout my public service in the state of Washington. MRSC's mission is to assist local governments in Washington in successfully serving their constituents by providing advice, research, and information to officials and staff of cities, counties, and special-purpose districts with a small team of professionals, many like me with years of experience to call upon.

During my career in public management I found value in using storytelling to illustrate a point or to empathize with others. These are some of my stories.

Lynn Nordby

I was encouraged to share my experiences and opinions through the MRSC web site, blog and publications. In addition I've been pleased to have had a few articles published in *Public Management*, the journal of the International City/County Management Association (ICMA). Over time I realized that I had accumulated quite a volume of written musings on the profession of public management.

I decided to assemble the individual pieces I've written into a single volume to share with my friends and colleagues in the profession some of the lessons learned and—I hope—a few chuckles from my experiences. The title, "Flying Lessons for Leaders and Managers: Notes on a Career in Local Government Management" is taken from one of my articles. Managing a public organization is often a lot like piloting an airplane: handling headwinds, crosswinds and the occasional tailwind while maintaining situational awareness and navigating your organization to reach its destination.

I'm grateful to MRSC and ICMA for permission to reuse material originally published by them.

Flying Lessons for Leaders and Managers

I've always been fascinated by powered flight. From the earliest days of aviation to the heroes who pushed the boundaries of technology or braved combat high above the earth, it has been a lifelong interest. I think every manager can use some "flying lessons" on the ground or in the air.

Fly the Plane

A friend of mine, a commercial airline pilot, described the circumstances of an airliner crash from a National Transportation Safety Board accident report. The investigation revealed that during the landing approach the entire cockpit crew had become fixated on a warning light that seemed to be on for no apparent reason. The aircraft had been set on autopilot at a fixed rate of descent and flew itself into the ground while both the pilot and co-pilot were distracted.

The lesson: somebody has to remember that their job is to "fly the plane." Even the most flat, participatory organizations ultimately have someone who has to make the final decision.

A continual search for more and better information can result in the "Paralysis of Analysis," overshooting the optimum point of decision making and resulting in a less desirable outcome. If you're in charge, you can't be distracted by operational details to the point of failing to lead. You need to understand what's going on around you and contribute where you can, but don't lose sight of the overall situation. Maintain situational awareness.

Set Priorities

The late U.S. Air Force Brigadier General Robin Olds, a World War II and Viet Nam "ace" fighter pilot, described what it was like in the cockpit of a jet fighter on a combat mission:

> Your senses were being assaulted by sights and sounds conveying information vital to your status, both offensively and defensively. Multiple audio signals told you your missile's radar was alert and whether your enemy's radar was trying to track you. At the same time, your eyes had to scan your instruments and the air and ground. Suddenly, surface to air missiles the size of telephone poles could be seen rising at supersonic speed toward you. Instinctively, you wanted to start weaving, hoping

they would all miss. But, the best way to avoid them was to systematically pick the most threatening one, dodge it, and then dodge the next one, and so on.

The lesson: set priorities, whether it's a threat you're dealing with or a project to manage. Avoid multi-tasking. Even though we all try to do many things simultaneously, every study of multi-tasking says it only makes us think that we're being more efficient. The fact is it's an illusion. Avoid being "shot down" by working from priorities you've set for yourself.

Don't Panic

In *The Right Stuff*, Tom Wolfe described the calm nature of the pilots who "pushed the envelope" in aviation. Flying untested aircraft that were often at the bleeding edge of technology, they were responsible for monitoring everything going on around them and being able to describe it by radio and in writing without benefit of the sophisticated digital equipment of today. When things went wrong, as they often did, only their systematic reporting provided clues for fixing the problem and for advancing the frontier. Wolfe described Chuck Yeager, the first man to break the sound barrier, as the archetype with his mellifluous southern drawl never sounding stressed, even when things around him were not going according to plan.

The lesson: as a leader, others will look to you to exhibit leadership qualities. In a crisis, your attitude alone can have a positive influence on those around you if you remain calm. This calmness also makes it easier to set the priorities necessary to organize the response to the situation.

Instincts Are Good—Training Is Better

Early aviation pioneers didn't have the benefit of instruments for flying at night or in bad weather; even an unexpected cloud bank could prove fatal. Relying on instincts and senses alone, many pilots died when they couldn't see. Instinct may serve as an early warning radar that something is wrong, but it doesn't necessarily tell you what to do. Training can. One city attorney I worked with for many years had been a naval aviator during the Viet Nam War. He related that, during pilot training, the seemingly petty requirement about maintaining your footlocker in the barracks didn't sink in until later when you were sitting on the aircraft carrier catapult. Then you realized that it wasn't about how you rolled your socks, it was about attention to detail.

The lesson: often your instincts will tell you when something "just isn't right." That's fine; but how do you know what to do? Whether it's an ethical question or a technical issue, you need training to know what to do about it. Merely reacting instinctively can make a bad situation worse. Training is available from many sources, often at no cost, through professional associations, risk management organizations, your agency's insurance carrier, online, or through the resources of MRSC. Through self-evaluation, you can identify areas where you may want additional training, and then look for it.

Do You Feel Lucky?

Pilots will probably tell you that in spite of all the training and experience, sometimes you're just plain lucky.

I wanted to reorganize my staff into what I believed would be much better alignment, making the best use of their abilities and reducing the number who directly reported to me. Unfortunately, among other things, it would require the demotion of one long-time, loyal, and capable manager. I didn't know how she would react, and I expected some resistance, or at best, hurt feelings. On the morning I'd decided to explain the plan to the staff, I found a letter on my desk from the affected manager announcing her decision to retire. There was no way she could have been aware of what I was planning. It was simply good fortune that allowed me to announce that with her retirement I would be making several changes in our organizational structure. Because I was prepared, I could capitalize on the opportunity without causing the pain I wished to avoid.

The lesson: be prepared. Even with a "Plan A" and a "Plan B," the unexpected may happen. If you're lucky, and it's a positive turn of events, so much the better. If not, you've got a better chance at organizational survival.

Perhaps these flying lessons can help you develop some of "the right stuff" for leadership.

Getting What You Want Through Foresight and Creativity: Part 1

You can't always get what you want . . . but I have found that sometimes you can, by using a little foresight and creativity.

Trees from Concrete

When I was city administrator, my city received some Federal Block Grant funds to extend sidewalks across a former railroad right-of-way. The intention was to improve pedestrian access and safety and encourage new development along a state highway running through town. We matched the Block Grant with our own funds from various sources to extend the project several additional blocks. We had no funds to include street trees in the project, but I asked the contractor to include square concrete sections, slightly thinner than the rest of the sidewalk, every thirty feet along the curb. These squares could be easily knocked out if we got the opportunity to plant trees at some later date.

Within a few weeks, I got a call from the Chamber of Commerce president asking what the "little squares" in the new sidewalk were for. When I told her, she said, "I thought so. Let me work on it."

She soon called to say that she had been seeking donated trees. Through her public-spirited efforts and others in the community, dozens of flowering cherry trees were donated, a local contractor provided the topsoil, the power company used a power pole auger to dig the holes, and volunteers from the Chamber of Commerce and Rotary Club planted the trees. All I had to do was have the city crew break out the "knock-outs" and cut a few more holes in some older sidewalks downtown.

On a single Saturday morning, the volunteers planted dozens of little cherry trees that have now grown and beautified the community for more than twenty years—all from just a few "knock-outs" put in the concrete when we had the chance.

The Fighting Seabees
On another occasion, the city received a grant for a community/senior center. The grant barely covered the purchase of a vacant building with a little left over for vinyl flooring and a small kitchen just to get the center started.

However, the city retained an architectural firm to prepare a long-range plan for more extensive renovations as soon as funds became available.

The young associate assigned to the project was very enthusiastic and developed a simple but pleasing plan. He mentioned that he was in the Naval Reserve, using his professional skills in a construction battalion (Seabee) unit. Sometimes they needed small indoor projects during the winter. He suggested I call his commanding officer.

I followed up as he suggested, and learned that they were looking for something right then. All I needed was a release from the unions that might otherwise have been involved in the project. This turned out to be surprisingly easy.

The end result was that we got all the wiring, plumbing, and framing (and most of the sheetrock) done by the Seabees for just the cost of materials. We were able to complete the project and provide a much more complete and functional community/senior center than we thought would be possible when we began the project.

Sometimes you need foresight and creativity to set up an opportunity; sometimes you need to take advantage of an opportunity presented to you. Either way, be the facilitator.

Great satisfaction in public service comes from seeing what foresight and creativity can do for your community.

R-E-S-P-E-C-T

After the Seattle Seahawks won Super Bowl XLVIII, much was written about the successful coaching style of Pete Carroll. From a leadership perspective, there are few, if any, better examples of effective leadership than coaching a Super Bowl victory. I even heard one on-air comment that Coach Carroll was "the boss everyone wishes they had." Is it any wonder that working individually with employees to improve their performance is commonly called "coaching"?

A few of the comments from and about Coach Carroll provide a mini-management seminar you can pull out of your pocket for a "halftime speech" to yourself when you need some encouragement as a leader.
Carroll says, "Of course we want to win every game, but winning forever is more about realizing your potential and making yourself as good as you can be. Realizing that is a tremendous accomplishment, whether it's in football or in life."

Just prior to the Super Bowl, Jerry Brewer of the *Seattle Times* wrote, "Carroll's greatest gift: the ability and willingness to get the best out of people who others would dismiss as too much trouble. Why does Carroll work so well with these flawed individuals? It's simple, the players say. He treats them with respect. He doesn't handle them differently. Carroll appeals to players' strengths, opens their eyes to the possibilities and challenges them to reach their potential."

Following the Seahawks' win, Doug Farrar of *Sports Illustrated* said, "[Carroll] believes in finding the best in the people around him and challenging them to find it at all times."

Carroll added, "I think that what we're talking about is the truth. Helping people be the best they can be—it doesn't matter what you're talking about. Football, or whether you're talking about business, or talking about families—the language and the intent and doing everything you can to help them. I can understand why that does resonate, and I'm very excited about that, because I know that the message goes beyond football."

The frequent reference to respect in leadership as a key ingredient in bringing out the best in others reminds me of an experience from my college days when I had the opportunity to spend an evening with the late Coach John Wooden from UCLA. Coach Wooden's success is unequaled. His teams were made up of future NBA stars as well as future actors, teachers, and city managers. He built his "Pyramid of Success" on statements of his coaching and leadership philosophies. "Respect" was part of the foundation. Not surprisingly, "respect" is also a key element in Carroll's "Win Forever" pyramid.

If you'd like to build a strong team, there is no better way than to begin with a foundation of respect.

Employee Satisfaction: What Goes Around Comes Around

Happy employees are goodwill ambassadors for your brand, whether it's selling a product or delivering public service. In his book *Extreme Government Makeover*, Ken Miller describes how improvements in systems that streamline workflow result in "better, faster, cheaper" public services.

Further evidence of the significance of satisfied employees to a positive bottom line was reported in American Public Media's Marketplace commentary in July. Teresa Amabile, Harvard Business School professor and the article's author, says "many…leaders undervalue respect. When faced with an employee's mistake, far too many rake the person over the coals. Research shows that respecting employees can help drive the bottom line upward. Doing the opposite can drive an enterprise into the ground."

In a recent article on NBCNews.com citing the worst companies to work for, one frequent consequence of employee dissatisfaction was poor customer service, which in turn resulted in financial losses for the company. Unhappy employees make for unhappy customers. "The terrible relationship these companies have with their employees often extends to their clientele as well. Most of the companies on this list are in industries that do poorly on customer satisfaction surveys," the article said. Some, like Sears and Radio Shack, frequently appear on lists of businesses predicted to soon disappear. While city halls or county courthouses don't suffer direct financial losses as a result of poor constituent relationships, the indirect consequences can damage the agency's reputation enough to be felt when they need voter support.

Reasons often cited at the core of employee dissatisfaction include archaic systems, disconnected management, years of layoffs, bad public relations, and high management turnover. Most of these factors sound like the issues faced by public sector employees.

What does this mean for public sector managers? Most important, treat your staff with respect. In a political and economic environment where there is small chance for any significant increase in compensation for public employees, look to the research cited by Miller in his book:

compensation *isn't* an effective motivator anyway. The majority of public employees are motivated by a desire to make a difference. You can have the greatest effect by attacking the de-motivators that frustrate and impede your employees' ability to do the jobs they want to do. Doing so will give them the best environment in which to improve their productivity and deliver better public service, often at little or no cost. That's within your power, regardless of what the economic or political barometer reads.

The Suggestion of the Year

In a *New York Times* "Corner Office" column interview with American Public Media Group founder and president emeritus Bill Kling, he was asked, "What have you learned about getting the most out of people?" His response: "Ask them… Watch carefully for who's doing something interesting but is very quiet and not promoting themselves." He went on to elaborate about the value of creative talents that people develop outside of work. I thought about an incident early in my career that illustrated the value of his advice.

The city operated a wastewater treatment plant that had been state of the art—before I was born! We were beginning preliminary studies about replacing the now-aging facility when the Public Works Supervisor said there indications that the pipes circulating hot water inside the digester (a large concrete tank containing thousands of gallons of sewage sludge) were leaking fresh water into the tank.

Without going into the details of secondary sewage treatment, let me just say that *this was a bad thing*, threatening the entire treatment process and the local environment. We immediately brought in our consulting engineers to analyze the situation and make recommendations for appropriate corrective action. They recommended installing a heat exchanger which would route the sludge out of the digester to be heated externally rather than trying to repair the heating coils inside the digester. This repair would require a shutdown of the tank and probably the entire treatment plant. Meanwhile every day that passed meant more and more fresh water was diluting the tank's contents, upsetting the biological process of breaking it down into more or less harmless fully digested sludge. In addition, the device would cost tens of thousands of dollars. And it would have to be manufactured to order and take a month to complete. Despite these drawbacks, we concluded that this was the way to go. We only hoped we could keep the plant going long enough.

Before starting the design, the engineers visited the site to determine the best location for the installation. The chief operator led the tour but didn't say much. After the engineers had left, he expressed some reservations. He was very reluctant to question the professional engineers, he said. After all, they were the professionals. He thought he'd have to just do the best he could. Nevertheless, he was concerned about being able to keep the treatment process going during the time it would take to get the heat exchanger designed, built, delivered, and installed. Though we had to press and encourage him to tell us what he really thought, he said he'd seen a homemade heat exchanger on a tour of another city's treatment plant. Without hesitation we sent him to get more information.

Within 24 hours he had photos and a sketch of a simple U-shaped pipe within a pipe set up so that the sludge was circulated through the central pipe while the larger outer pipe was filled with heated water. Valves on the ends of the "U" regulated the flow to make sure it transferred enough heat. We asked our engineers if it would work. When they confirmed that it would, we contracted with a local welding shop to build it. In a week it was up and running for less than 10% of the original estimate for a manufactured heat exchanger. The quick installation saved the ongoing treatment process from being disrupted, thereby preventing untold negative environmental damage in addition to whatever economic impact some sort of temporary sewage interruption might have had on the local economy. Not to mention the simple cost effectiveness of this solution.

That improvised heat exchanger continued to serve the plant effectively until a completely new wastewater treatment facility was brought online eight years later. So, not only was this a cost-effective and timely repair, but since we were in the planning stages for a new sewage treatment facility, the employee's suggestion saved a significant expense for what would have been only a short-term need. These funds were better spent in the long run on the design of the new plant.

Not only did I get a condensed lesson in secondary sewage treatment, I also learned a valuable lesson in management. Some of your most valuable resources are the people performing the daily tasks of public service. The practical knowledge they've gained should not be overlooked in problem solving. Be alert to subtle cues your staff may give. Not all will be quick to come forward with a suggestion. You may have to coax a "minority report" out of someone that will wind up as the suggestion of the year, or even the decade.

Big Results with a Small Gesture

Sometimes a small gesture of appreciation can generate lasting benefits.

The study session with the city council seemed to last forever. As the city administrator, I delivered a report on a policy issue involving a utility owned and operated by the city. The city council had a lot of questions. They weren't particularly hostile—just detailed and thorough, as they should be. I was on center stage for two or three hours responding to the questions.

As is often the case with public policy issues, the matter wasn't resolved that night. That can be hard to accept, especially when you've put a lot into preparing a major recommendation.

The next day, a councilmember stopped by my office. Since I was out, he left a note: "You did a great job last night."

I saved it for a long time. I've forgotten the details of the issue, but that small gesture has stayed with me. I've used this anecdote countless times while mentoring and coaching staff members in how to motivate and reward their employees. Empirical research has repeatedly shown that monetary rewards are not the most effective means of motivation. I can surely attest to that.

Managers need to use this kind of appreciation for their employees. With monetary resources increasingly scarce (and less effective anyway), extending a simple "Good job!" to let people know they and their work are valued is now more important than ever. I assure you, they will remember it.

See Something? Say Something

No doubt we've all seen a poster bearing the admonition, "See Something, Say Something." It's a wonderfully simple catchphrase no doubt conceived to encourage the general populace to be aware of potential dangers around them. It occurred to me that this clever saying could be put to use as an organizational admonition for both leaders and employees. Here are five ways it can help build stronger, more effective organizations.

1. Give Praise

I firmly believe in the long-term effectiveness of even small expressions of appreciation from leaders toward those who work for and with them. *See something? Say something.* Give feedback immediately. When you see good work being done, let the employee know. They will appreciate both the acknowledgement and the fact that it was even noticed. By responding immediately you also reduce the possibility that it might be forgotten before a more formal performance evaluation comes due.

2. Give Constructive Criticism

The same value applies to negative feedback as well. Sometimes we witness substandard behavior. It's best not to "let it slide," but instead *see something, say something.* Depending on the severity of the breach it doesn't have to be a big deal, just a note or comment with a suggestion for improvement. This may be all that it takes to prevent a major issue later. I still remember a brief conversation early in my career with the assistant city manager. Following a difficult planning commission meeting, he offered both corrective advice and support. I knew what I needed to do next time, but I also knew he would be there to back me up if I needed it.

3. Deliver More

For those not in a leadership position the same catchphrase is equally applicable. *See something? Say something.* An effective team is more than just each member doing what's expected of them according to their job description. Maximum effectiveness comes from exceeding expectations. One of my "pet peeves" is when I see a pothole just beyond the end of a new paving job. The crew could have easily thrown a couple of shovels of asphalt into it but simply ignored it because it wasn't part of the job. "It's not my job" is simply an unacceptable response at any time.

4. Speak the Truth

"Silos"—departments or divisions kept apart and discouraged from collaborating by policy or custom—severely weaken organizations. Most organizational development literature agrees that the "tone at the top" is largely responsible for the creation of these "silos," but employees following the *See something? Say something* model can take the initiative and "speak truth to power." Tell the boss that silos are present and are creating a barrier to becoming a high-performance organization.

5. Be a Hero

We're all inspired by accounts of heroes who go "above and beyond" to help someone else. Look for ways to be an organizational hero. If you *see something* that's out of your area of expertise but still within the realm of your organization's responsibility, take it upon yourself to *say something* by passing it on to someone who can deal with it. It's easy to assume that the right person will come along any minute and take care of it. But don't take the easy way out and make that assumption. If you get a question you can't handle, make sure it gets directed to someone who can.

Getting What You Want Through Foresight and Creativity: Part 2

Earlier I described how a significant volunteer civic beautification effort was inspired by the inclusion of "knock-out" panels for future tree wells in a new sidewalk project. I briefly mentioned that the HUD Block Grant was matched with funds from "various sources."

I'd like to offer a couple of examples of sources for matching grant funds and how those funds extended local dollars in creative ways.

The above-mentioned project extended sidewalks across an abandoned railroad right-of-way adjacent to a state highway right-of-way. The city water utility also maintained water lines constructed along the route of some of the railroad tracks without regard to the current street location. Some of the former railroad right-of-way was now private property and the location, age, and condition of the water lines were a liability for both the city and the property owners. Relocating the water lines from the private property into the nearest street right of way, which was a state highway, would require considerable added costs and complications for permitting, traffic control, highway closures, and restoration to state highway standards. However, the state department of transportation did not consider the area outside the curb line to be their jurisdiction.

The existing sidewalks were in a terrible state of disrepair. They were broken, sunken below grade, and trapped storm water when it rained—*and outside the state's jurisdiction.* I decided we should build the new water line under the sidewalk instead of under the street. The cost to the water fund for replacing the old, broken sidewalk by matching and extending the grant-funded sidewalk project was more than offset by savings realized by not having to meet the requirements of working in the state's portion of the right-of-way. A new water line on public property replaced the deteriorated old line that was a liability and an obstacle to redevelopment, *and* several blocks of new pedestrian access were created. The finished project included money from the block grant, current expenses, and street and water funds.

The second example involved a badly deteriorated major sewer interceptor extending for several blocks under a neighborhood street. The street itself was also in poor condition: without curbs, gutters, or a functioning storm water collection system. Due to the interceptor's depth, the excavation for its replacement meant that virtually the entire existing street surface would be destroyed and need to be replaced.

Since we had adequate lead time, we were able to work with the neighborhood to form a local improvement district to add curbing and storm drains to the project and include them in the bidding specifications for the interceptor replacement. Grant money and the required city match for the interceptor and pavement restoration paid for the paving, and the property owners had only to pick up the incremental cost of the curbs and drainage collection. Working with the neighborhood in the process resulted in a much better finished product at a significantly reduced cost to the property owners.

Easy and Effective Common-sense Risk Management

Managing risk for your agency doesn't always require sophisticated or expensive systems or extra staff resources. Sometimes a few simple, low-cost, common-sense procedures can be implemented to protect your organization from liability.

Enjoying one of the city's parks with my family, I noticed that one of the swing seats (the flexible sling type) appeared to have some cracks in it. I asked one of our maintenance people to inspect it and see if it should be replaced. The employee reported that the swing I mentioned and several others were in poor condition, even though to a casual observer they looked safe. In one, the metal band that reinforced the rubber seat had cracked nearly all the way through!

I immediately authorized the replacement of all the flexible swing seats and all the "s" hooks at the top of the chains that took most of the wear. I also ordered that all the swings be inspected every Monday morning and that the inspection results be noted on a simple log. I further authorized the replacement of the flexible swing seats every year prior to the heavy summer use, whether they appeared to need it or not. I decided that new seats were cheaper than a potential injury.

The staff faithfully followed this documented inspection, maintenance, and replacement routine for several years.

A few years later, an adult using a swing was injured when it broke and the person fell to the ground. The city's liability insurer denied the claim for damages, and the city was subsequently sued. The city's motion to have the suit dismissed cited, among other things, the regular, documented inspections and maintenance of the swing sets during the previous several years. The motion was granted, undoubtedly saving the taxpayers much more than the cost of inspecting and replacing a few swing seats every year.

Most risk management can be summarized as good common sense. It can be made even more effective with a few simple steps:

- Record what maintenance steps are followed and when
- Record what remedial actions are taken and when
- Take pictures (the digital record will document when they were taken).

The Sharpest Tools in the Shed

"To be a part of a throwaway mentality that discards goods and ideas, that discards principles and law, that discards persons and families, is to be at the dying edge." – Max Depree, *Leadership Is an Art*

This quotation seems appropriate to open a discussion of public sector leadership as many jurisdictions face staff reductions. Public service is, by definition, a service industry. The majority of the budget of most public agencies is for the salaries of the people who deliver the services. With the dramatic and prolonged decline of local government revenue it was inevitable that workers' wages, hours, working conditions, and benefits would be impacted. Even as the general economy recovers from the so-called Great Recession the negative effects on local government revenue continue to be felt. How we make decisions and treat the people directly affected by budget and staff reductions, whether through attrition, layoffs, or furloughs will determine whether or not we're at the "dying edge."

It's a reasonable analogy to say that people are the "tools" of public service. The aphorism, "It's a poor workman who blames his tools" dates from the Middle Ages and expresses a basic truth that can be applied to public management. Public leaders and managers are responsible for the way we utilize the tools we're trusted with. We implement policies and programs with these human "implements." While the origins of "Take good care of your tools and they'll take good care of you" are unclear, the meaning is clear to any craftsman. If you've misused your tools or failed to maintain them properly, they won't serve you well when you need them. As a community leader you're responsible for how sharp your tools are as well as how well you use them. Your ability to motivate and inspire is even more important now than when the city or county's coffers are flush. This is a critical time to show respect and empathy for the staff that are bearing the brunt of the effects of cost-cutting measures.

Critics of government may be quick to equate the reductions in force to "cutting fat" and "something that should have happened long before." Resist the temptation to agree with them even if you do. For employees losing their jobs and those still serving the public, such expressions demean them and belittle their service.

While at the moment "taking good care" of your personnel probably doesn't include monetary rewards, if you do your best for the people who work for you in other respects they are much more likely to do their best for you. This can be as simple as showing interest in what they do, sincerely involving them in finding solutions,[1] and showing respect.

Those still on the job are likely to be fearful and demoralized. It's your job to minimize the factors that contribute to those feelings and take whatever steps are within your ability to maintain morale. Don't miss an opportunity to recognize the good work of your staff. Praise for major accomplishments is always appropriate and appreciated. So is recognition for doing the everyday tasks to maintain continuity of your agency's public services.

It shouldn't be a surprise that even employees who are relieved to have survived the latest round of budget cuts may be experiencing survivor's guilt. They're happy to still be employed but sad to lose coworkers with whom they've shared a large part of their daily lives.

The loss of coworkers may even make your remaining employees experience grief symptoms such as those described by Elisabeth Kubler-Ross: denial, anger, bargaining, depression, and acceptance.[2] Recognizing that your employees will be going through similar emotions gives you the opportunity to anticipate and actively deal with them. Having an employee assistance program available can be helpful for those coping with conflicting emotions.

While the overall economy may have officially turned the corner, it is generally agreed that state and local governments will have to endure more difficult budget cycles as any recovery of government revenue traditionally lags behind personal and business income growth. Furthermore, various tax limitation measures in recent years have reset the tax base in a way that structurally guarantees that the recovery will be even slower.

Anticipating that the times of difficult budgeting are not over, how can we keep our "tools" sharp?

· Know what to expect. People will feel fear, anger, sadness and grief. Have the means to handle it.
· Treat people the way you'd want to be treated: with respect, fairness, openness, and honesty.
· Show appreciation. It doesn't cost anything and yet yields lasting results.

---

1. "Survivors indicated that they were reassured when they could understand and could have a voice in the restructuring process. They expressed frustration when their input was not sought or

when it was ignored to the detriment of the organization." From "Survivors of downsizing: helpful and hindering experiences.*" Career Development Quarterly,* Monday, March 1, 2004.

2. "How to Cope When Coworkers Lose Their Jobs: Layoff Survivors Experience Feelings of Guilt, Sadness, Loss, and Fear." http://humanresources.about.com/od/layoffsdownsizing/a/survivors _cope.htm

This article originally appeared in the ICMA publication Public Management *under the title "Maintain the Sharpest Tools." Used with permission.*

The Flood

I was nine years old when my father was appointed as the city manager of the Alaska town where I was born and spent my childhood. It was his first city manager job and I didn't know what a city manager did. I had no idea how quickly I would learn about the closeness of the link between city management and personal life.

Every summer during my childhood, Dad and I would go on a camping trip, usually somewhere easily accessible by car—just a father/son getaway, cooking over an open fire, sleeping in the car or on the ground, and enjoying the outdoors. Our camping trip that summer was the weekend just after Dad's appointment. As we headed out of town Friday afternoon, dark storm clouds were gathering on the horizon. We joked about outrunning them, hoping they wouldn't follow us and spoil our outing.

We thought we were pretty lucky since we outran the storm and had a great time. Little did we know—in those days before instant communication—that we'd outrun the storm because it parked itself over the city and dumped torrential rains there for 48 hours. The first public works terminology I learned turned out to be "combined storm and sanitary sewer." The city had such a system, some of which dated to the time of Alaska's gold rush. The storm had overwhelmed it, causing sewer backups all over town. Virtually every basement was flooded, including ours—and the new city manager was out of town.

When we got home, Mom was coping with a two-foot flood of sewage in our basement as well as the *flood* of calls for Dad. I still remember him wondering out loud whether he might just be the shortest-term city manager in history. As it turned out, the city council understood that the storm wasn't something Dad could have foreseen nor done much about even if he had been home. His city management career didn't end there after all.

When the crisis had passed, I still didn't know exactly what Dad did as city manager. But at the age of nine I learned how events in the community could have an impact on our home life in a way far different than in any other home in town.

With today's communications technology, it's inconceivable that a city manager would be out of touch during an emergency like that flood. We are in constant contact whether we want it or not. The benefit to our communities is undeniable. No matter where we are, we can be called upon for advice or decision making.

At the same time you need to be cognizant of the toll that being in constant contact can have on your health and family. If you're really on vacation, you should delegate authority to someone who can act in your stead. You probably can't effectively manage a crisis from the far side of the world anyway.

Municipal Budgeting at the Age of Nine

My introduction to municipal budgeting came at the age of nine when my Dad was appointed City Manager of Fairbanks, Alaska. At the time all I knew was that we weren't going to be seeing much of him for a while during the budget review and adoption process. As a small compensation, we'd get to enjoy some of the things for dinner we liked and Dad didn't. Little did I realize that just fifteen years later I'd be on my own as a new City Administrator with my first city budget to prepare.

More than thirty city budgets later, I'd like to share some thoughts with the many dedicated public officials—elected and appointed—who'll be preparing their own.

It is often said that "The Devil is in the details." When it comes to budgets, however, details can be "too much of a good thing." Certainly a useful budget needs many detailed ideas. All too often, though, a sharp focus on the details of a line-item budget can lose sight of "El Photo Grande," The Big Picture. Sometimes it helps to step back from all the detail, put your eyes into soft focus, look at the department or program under consideration as a whole, and ask a simple question: "Are we (am I) satisfied in general with the performance and services delivered by this program or department?" Once you've answered this question it's easier to identify and deal with the issues necessary to bring the program into line with your expectations.

After I had been with one city for a number of years, a senior City Council member asked me why we examined every department's budget line by line. Often the Council was already satisfied with the department's performance. The only questions seemed to be routine inquiries about details having little to do with the overall mission and function of the department. He suggested that the Council ask that threshold question of each department first. If they believed the departmental budget as proposed was reasonable and in line with expectations, they would simply move on to consideration of the next department/program.

Those "ifs" are big! We're back to the details again. For the City Council to have that kind of confidence in the city staff, there must be an *earned* level of trust and experience between the staff and elected officials. It doesn't just happen. It's incumbent on the staff to build the budget that is submitted with careful attention to details that the elected officials won't necessarily scrutinize but for which they will nevertheless be responsible. The staff must be prepared with sufficient detailed information to answer any question that may arise just as they would if the budget was being reviewed at that level of detail.

When we tried it for the first time the following year, we discussed the process with the City Council beforehand and agreed that we would have as much detail available in reserve for all city operations as we would have had for a line-item review. We wanted to be able to answer any question that might arise and we wanted the Council to feel assured that we had anything they needed if they wanted it. In addition to a very simplified numerical budget in our presentation to the Council, we included a series of issue papers for new programs or additional staff positions. These issue papers clearly described what differed from the previous year in both cost and operation. If the Council chose to delete any of these proposals, it was simple to subtract it from the bottom line for that department. The Council knew what was being proposed and what it cost. Instead of focusing time and energy going over the details of a budget for a department they already knew and understood, they spent their time on what was going to make a difference.

The result: a budget process that had taken several hours a night for several nights the previous year was reviewed in one evening in less than two hours!

The ability to achieve a smooth budget process is based on mutual trust. Early in my career, I would spend much of my budget preparation time cutting department requests so I could submit a preliminary budget to the City Council that stayed within projected revenue. Department directors routinely submitted budget requests for more than they expected in the hope that the final budget would be sufficient or maybe even have a little extra for new programs or unexpected contingencies. This left me with the drudgery of balancing the budget and the directors with the fear that I'd cut something really important to them. This was a waste of our time, so I made a deal with them: Submit a realistic budget and I'll be with you in front of the Council to ask for more if you come up short, but snow me and you're on your own. It worked! On the first try we had a budget that was within projected revenues!

Later in my career, several statewide initiatives had complicated the revenue picture and seriously reduced our options. The city's department directors asked if they could work together on their own to see if they could submit a budget balanced both in sum and between their interests before they submitted it to me. They produced a draft budget that stayed within projected revenue and dramatically reduced the amount of unnecessary effort involved in preparing the preliminary budget.

There's a definite pattern in these examples: *trust and confidence*. When these elements are present the entire process is improved, resulting in more effective use of time and resources, less stress, and better service to the public.

Birch Hill

My father was appointed City Manager of Fairbanks, Alaska in 1958 when I was still in elementary school. That's when my education about municipal government began.

Delivering public services presented unique challenges in the far north, especially in winter when temperatures reached minus-60 degrees and the ground was frozen as hard as concrete. Some were hazardous and others simply "unique."

Fairbanks was truly a full-service city, providing not only the usual services you'd expect but also the telephone system and even steam heat to several commercial buildings from excess generated by the city-operated electrical power generators.

Another enterprise was the Birch Hill Cemetery.

Upon entering the cemetery, the drive went straight up a fairly steep hill. For some time the City Council had considered building a new entry through the forest on another part of the property that would permit a more gently sloping road up the hill through an attractive and quiet birch grove. It was considered more aesthetic than practical and therefore a low funding priority.

Events have a way of intervening to change priorities. One day a funeral procession proceeded solemnly up the steep hill. About halfway up the slope, the latches retaining the casket in the hearse came loose. It slid backward into the door and knocked it open. To the shock of the mourners, the casket rolled down the drive and came to rest in front of the next car in the procession.

The City Council authorized funds for a new road through the peaceful birch forest at the next meeting.

The frozen earth was another consideration. Municipal water systems had to avoid dead-end lines so the water would keep circulating and not freeze. Lines to individual houses had to go in and back out again. Sewer lines were made of wood (in the days before modern plastics) to provide some insulation from the frozen ground and allow for flexibility as the earth thawed and refroze.

Every autumn, before the top few feet of soil that had warmed during the long summer days froze again, the public works crew estimated how many grave sites might be needed during the coming winter and dug several in advance.

One winter they underestimated. After using the last pre-dug site, the crew had to excavate every succeeding grave inch by inch using a jackhammer. Eventually the conditions caught up with them. They couldn't complete one excavation in time for a funeral procession. The crew cleared an area around the shallow indentation they'd made in the rock-hard earth for a brief graveside committal service in the time remaining in the short sub-arctic day. After the participants left, the crew moved the casket to a storage building and decided to ease the work of completing the excavation the following day by trying to thaw the ground overnight. They filled the shallow trench with wood and old tires, doused them with diesel fuel, ignited the fuel and left for the day, expecting that the heat would thaw the soil enough to permit a quick completion of the burial the following day.

No one expected the family to return in the morning.

A smoldering pile of ashes lay where they had last seen the casket! After frantic and angry phone calls, the family was reassured that the casket had been safely and respectfully stored while the crew tried to deal with the frozen ground.

Delivering public service requires not only good management and organizational and political skills but also diplomacy, compassion, grief counseling, and a sense of humor.

Strength Out of Stress: The Refiner's Fire

(To readers: I wrote this during the Great Recession. While parts may seem outdated, I believe that it contains some valuable lessons)

I've always held a somewhat organic view of systems and organizations, seeing examples in nature that illustrate how people and institutions respond to the things that happen around and to them.

- Trees that grow up in a forest surrounded by other trees are less able to resist a strong wind than trees that grow up exposed to strong winds year after year.

- Muscles get stronger only when repeatedly stressed through exercise.

- Precious metals must be melted in a crucible over a refiner's fire so impurities are either burned away or rise to the surface where they can be skimmed off as slag.

- Annealing soft metals by hammering and heating them changes the molecular structure to make them harder or more resilient.

- Some seeds only germinate after exposure to fire.

If these analogies hold true with institutions, as I believe they do, local government can emerge from this stressful period stronger and more focused than ever. As hard as it may be to accept the demise of projects or programs you've successfully provided in the past, the heritage of your public service will live on. For example, I recently heard that operation of the municipal cemetery in a community I once served was to be contracted to the local funeral home. While I was there we were proud to operate it "in the black" for many years. Apparently that's no longer the case.

If a project or program truly has merit, it will survive in its new form. We didn't enter public service to build a personal legacy. If some public services must be contracted to another agency or the private sector to maintain efficiency, what matters is that the public is still served. The heritage is still there. What we were proud of before is still valuable and still exists in its new form. The accomplishments of the past established the service in the first place and made it possible to hand something over to new management now.

The news brings story after story about the loss of state and local revenue and the resultant reductions in services and layoffs or furloughs of public employees. Very few localities escaped the effects of the Great Recession, which caused such precipitous drops in the revenue that severe cuts had to be made from the levels they were prior to the collapse.

It can be hard to accept when accomplishments, projects, and programs you've been responsible for or personally taken part in are considered for cancellation or outsourcing to another agency or the private sector. Services once considered so successful they were highlighted on our resumes are now highlighted as "unsustainable" and "marked for termination" as we once knew them.

There has been some improvement in the economy. Fewer applications for unemployment benefits are being filed; more cars and houses are being sold. Some believe, optimistically, that things can and will return to some version of "normal." After all, didn't we have a pretty strong economy before investment banks and hedge funds began playing fast and loose? Won't it be possible to return to a level of economic stability and prosperity though not quite as superheated as it was before it melted? Maybe that will be the "new normal." We can reinstitute the programs and services we proudly offered to our citizens, though perhaps at a slightly reduced level.

Maybe not.

First, most analysts predict that even with the national economic recovery it could take years to see a recovery in local government revenue. On top of that, even though federal taxes are actually at the lowest level in 60 years, the anti-tax movement seems stronger and louder than ever. We know that there will be growing tax revenue needs at the national level as the "baby boom" generation begins claiming its Social Security and Medicare benefits, not to mention the uncertain future cost of current or future health-care reform initiatives. Finally, previous tax cutting measures which set a new, much lower ceiling on local revenues with a built-in "growth" factor of 1% or the rate of inflation—whichever is less—have resulted in an even lower starting point for recovery and will all but guarantee that local government revenue will probably be in a hole for a long, long time.

Unlike a private enterprise that has the option of simply closing its doors, public services have to carry on in the face of economic reality. Critics simplistically demand cuts in "waste." Years after Proposition 13 was passed in California, one of the criticisms of the state's response was that the state provided funds to local governments to make up the lost revenue. The public didn't perceive any of the drastic consequences predicted by its opponents. Here in Washington, Initiative 695, repealing the Motor Vehicle Excise Tax (overturned in court then subsequently reinstated through legislation) was responded to in much the same way. The state temporarily provided "backfill" payments to the most heavily impacted jurisdictions and, combined with the real estate "bubble," the real structural defects of local government finances were disguised until the results of the huge tax cut were no longer seen as a cause and effect by the general public. In several cities I'm aware of, the annual loss of sales tax equalization (funded by the MVET) ranged from nearly a million dollars to almost four million dollars a year. That would have gone a long way toward plugging the holes in Current Expense funds, to keep up with basic services like street maintenance, public safety, and prevent furloughs. But in the late 1990s and early 2000s the true impact was hardly noticed. The impact on smaller communities, though of less magnitude, was just as devastating.

Any hope of gaining local support for new tax revenue will require convincing voters that the value of local services outweighs the added cost. The British call it "value for money," a pretty straightforward expression of the principle.

One of my colleagues once said that trying to find the fat in the city budget was like trying to find fat in hamburger. With care, the transition to alternate forms or methods of service delivery will respect the efforts of the past to build the communities we enjoy today while the "fat" is rendered out of the "hamburger." The result will be smaller local government. If the process has been open and the consequences fully understood, local government should also be more credible in the eyes of its citizens. The challenge for many has been to continue to provide public services in the face of a persistent erosion of local revenue. Discretionary expenditures are deferred or cancelled and essential services are reduced to minimal acceptable levels. Openness and candor in the process and about the consequences can help avoid the detachment of cause from effect as reported about Proposition 13 in California and may have contributed to further anti-tax measures here following I-695.

As local governments search for remedies such as outsourcing or discontinuing certain services altogether, we need to keep in mind that simply shifting the responsibility to someone else may not be the final answer.

UPS and FedEx are often held up against the US Postal Service for comparison. As easy as it is to bash the Postal Service, neither UPS nor FedEx has the mandate to serve every address, every business day. They take only a fraction of the freight, charge a premium, and size their staffs and fleets accordingly. Public services aren't always the most efficient due to their mandates. Private providers may end up being unable to make a profit under those conditions. Public agencies may be called upon to step forward again in the interest of public service.

From this economic crucible some strength may emerge.

Externally – Working with community groups and leaders of the business community, we may be able to identify and recruit businesses that enhance the local mix and broaden our economic base. New volunteers or candidates for appointed positions or elective office may be drawn to service by local needs.

Internally – Restructuring job descriptions and responsibilities that have hindered creativity, responsibility, and flexibility will lead to a more efficient and responsive organization. Process improvements that promote maximum performance by eliminating unproductive, redundant procedures that cost time and money and add little value will reap long-term dividends.

Fiscally – The structural defects of local government finance are being exposed. If we've been open and candid in our response we stand a better likelihood of having them acknowledged and rectified. For example, in 2010 the state legislature responded with ESHB 3179 which repealed non-supplanting requirements in previously authorized local option taxes and addressed the impacts of the adverse court decision on taxing brokered natural gas.

Politically – Responsible local action taken openly with an honest representation of the consequences builds credibility with the public. If you promise dire consequences, they need to be delivered as surely as good ones do. Sugarcoating problems associated with the cuts that need to be made only creates a trap to deal with later on. In the end, if the economy can't deliver the revenues to support the level of services, it will be up to the public to approve restructured tax systems or accept the level of services the present system can support.

"Close Enough for Government Work"

There are always words or catchphrases that capture people's imaginations and seem to be just the right shorthand to express a thought or make a point. After a while, though, they lose their impact through overuse. They are no longer clever and need to be retired. I don't need another "wake-up call" unless I'm in a hotel and might miss my flight, nor do I want to "take it to the next level" unless I'm on the "up" escalator. CEFGW is one expression that I want to eradicate from our lexicon forever.

I was enjoying an afternoon working with a friend on an old car—not the kind that could justify an expensive restoration, just a nice old "driver" he was fixing up—when he used the expression to indicate that he'd gotten whatever it was he was working on into acceptable shape to reinstall. I stopped him immediately and asked him not to use that expression around me again, *ever*. At first I think he thought I was kidding but I told him emphatically that that expression insulted and offended me.

That was the first time I'd ever spoken up about it but it wasn't the last. Like all such expressions it evokes an image that the speaker and the hearer can quickly absorb without further elaboration. Just like a racial slur, it depends on stereotyping for effect.

But also like racial stereotyping, it does a disservice to the vast majority of the people it lumps into a single category. Just imagine if the CEFGW stereotype were truly representative of these professions: police detective, firefighter, paramedic, crossing guard, prison guard, public health nurse, restaurant inspector, traffic engineer, air traffic controller, prosecutor, accountant, meter reader, water treatment operator, auditor, SWAT team, and many more.

My experience with "customer service" at many businesses tempts me to coin a new phrase like "Close Enough for the Private Sector," but that would be just as wrong.

With any denigrating process, an unfortunate byproduct is for the targets of the slur to "live down" to the stereotype, willing to accept what others expect to see. As leaders and managers we work diligently to motivate and inspire the people in our organizations to serve the public efficiently and effectively, now more than ever. We have to fight any tendency to accept less than the best and defend the reputation of people we lead.

Next time you hear that expression, speak up. Don't let it go without a response. Maybe we can make it just as unacceptable as any other insult based on stereotyping and crude generalization.

And while we're at it, can we get rid of "wake-up call" too?

"Be Sure You're Right, Then Go Ahead"

This quote was attributed to Davy Crockett in the 1950s Disney television series. It was a simple moral lesson for young viewers absorbed in the adventures of Fess Parker in his coonskin cap portraying the legendary 19th century frontiersman.

Like so many other words of wisdom, it encapsulates, in a simple phrase, a broader concept that often can be easier said than done, particularly in the realm of managing the daily implementation of public policy.

Much public policy has more to do with the perspective of the policymakers than with right and wrong. Although they may firmly believe that they are "right" when a majority on the governing body makes a final decision on an issue, those on the opposite side of the issue are equally convinced of the "rightness" of their position. Researchers think there are measurable differences in the way people view and absorb the exact same sets of facts or events that lead them to adopt partisan positions. Community members share these same traits. For the staff and managers charged with implementation of public policies, this can be a challenge.

The way supposedly objective and subjective elements of public policy intertwine can create a "perfect storm" of disagreement as to just what is "right."

Ponder these real world examples and observations that illustrate the challenges.

Mother, May I?

In an effort to avoid liability for taking private property through regulation, the city council included a number of "bonuses" that could be applied by a developer to gain back density otherwise lost through various setbacks and reserves required to protect environmentally sensitive areas on the site. At the end of the ordinance section, the council added a caveat to advise prospective applicants that, even if they took advantage of all the available bonuses, it might not be possible to regain the full density possible from a similarly sized but unencumbered piece of property. Unfortunately all the ordinance actually said was something like "You may not achieve the full density."

Fast forward a few years. We received a project application that attempted, with some success, to observe all the various required setbacks and reserves and still put the same number of units on the site. Opponents of the project read the code and concluded that "You *may not* achieve the full density…" was an absolute: "You *shall not*…" The staff processed the application with the understanding that the city council meant it as a caveat, not a mandate, and the opponents strongly argued the opposite. They maintained that the applicant would not be allowed to achieve the maximum underlying density equivalent to a piece of similar but unencumbered piece of property *under any circumstances*, regardless of the steps they took to protect the environmentally sensitive areas on the property. Eventually some sort of compromise was reached but not before a lot of negative energy was expended with the staff taking a great deal of criticism and mistrust.

Regardless of one's point of view on the issue itself, all of this could have been avoided by adopting clearer, more specific language in the first place.

Sand in the Gears
A procedural mistake can derail even the most worthy proposal. Whether it's the criminal justice system or a rezone application, the rights of the various parties are guaranteed by local, state and national laws. Failure to observe the letter of the law as well as the spirit, as in the appearance of fairness doctrine, must be avoided. Mistakes

may happen but if your local ordinances are so difficult to understand that procedures are confusing or hard to follow, the chances for a mistake are multiplied. A sophisticated constituency knows how to bring a process to a halt just by claiming a procedural misstep.

The Empty Hearing Room

When no one appeared at the public hearing on a particular project, a board member opposed to the project asserted that the hearing notices must not have been mailed (when in fact they had), resulting in a 30-day delay so the mailing could be verified.

Whose Woods Are These?

The municipal code in another city required that a notice be posted "on the property" in addition to notices mailed to surrounding property owners. The applicant's site was within a larger undeveloped wooded site. The posted hearing notice was inadvertently erected near but not actually on the applicant's property. This procedural misstep resulted in another delay and unfounded accusations from both the applicant and project opponents that it was somehow done intentionally.

Full Circle

Using circular logic, an opponent of a project allowed under the codes in effect filed a proposal to amend the comprehensive plan to make such projects illegal. The opponent then challenged the validity of continuing to process the application on the grounds that a comp plan amendment was "pending."

What's the "Right" Thing to Do?

When adopting and implementing laws and policies, take the extra time to make sure the intent is clear and that implementation and enforcement are achievable. You don't have to get into the specifics of the policy to ask the staff to look for obvious pitfalls before you take the final vote.

With the benefit of hindsight, it's easy to see how a few easy modifications to the notice requirements and agenda packets could have avoided some of these situations.

As the chief executive or manager within the organization, you are responsible for the performance of the staff. Unclear, unenforceable policies inhibit individual and organizational performance.

A common organizational response is to develop "workarounds": adaptations to unclear, anomalous, or simply stupid procedures. Like the layers of an onion, these steps accrete and before you know it the process is bogged down by seemingly unknown forces. A procedure adopted to respond to a particular incident stays in place long after whatever precipitated the incident is no longer an issue. I remember the caption from a cartoon in my building inspector's office: "There's no reason for it, it's just our policy." Don't let that be your motto.

Be aware of this natural tendency. Use process-improvement techniques and involve the staff to analyze the way your organization gets things done. As I've said before, "Assume nothing—It's probably not as good as it seems." The staff appreciate being able to contribute to process improvement, and they're the real experts anyway. Clearing obstacles that inhibit your employees' best performance is an important aspect of effective leadership.

Getting What You Want Through Foresight and Creativity: Part 3

Rezoning the "Triangle" for "Super Non-conforming Uses"

Envision a sizable triangle-shaped area in the center of the city, bounded on two sides by state highways and on the third by a little-used railroad right-of-way parallel to the central business district. The frontage along the first highway was zoned for automobile-oriented businesses, and for light industrial use along the second side and in the center. The city's central business district lay beyond the third side.

Over the years several recommendations had been made to rezone the "triangle," allowing new commercial users to infill between the downtown and the highway. Unfortunately a few influential light-manufacturing business owners always persuaded the City Council to leave the zoning "as is." As a result, two separate commercial areas—the old downtown and a newer highway-oriented district—gradually evolved. In between, along the other street and inside the "triangle" itself, there was a mixture of businesses that didn't relate either to downtown or the highway-oriented businesses. We'd had no interest from light industrial firms in locating there. In fact, the only new developments had been a restaurant and a garden store.

Our Planning Director and I concluded that the only way to ensure future investment in the "triangle" and avoid perpetuating a divided commercial core was to revisit the previously unsuccessful rezone recommendations and make them compatible with the adjacent commercial zoning. We realized we'd face the same objections from the light-manufacturing businesses that felt threatened by becoming non-conforming users.

When an area is rezoned, customarily the land uses that don't fit in the new zone become "non-conforming" when an area is rezoned. The intent is that they'll eventually go away or at least become less significant as new "conforming" uses surround them. They're usually restricted from expansion or remodeling beyond a certain limited percentage. If destroyed for any reason they either may not rebuild or must do so within a limited time period.

We realized that this custom posed an unacceptable threat to the business/property owners. It could even make their business financing difficult. We decided to recommend a different approach to "non-conforming."

We drafted a new definition for non-conforming uses in the "triangle" that allowed expansion and remodeling. They would be limited to the property owned at the time of the rezone. In addition, they could completely tear down and replace their facility or rebuild after a disaster within a generous time period without being "zoned out." The principal stipulation was that any new use had to conform to the new zoning.

Prior to making the recommendation public, we met individually with the affected property owners to explain the proposal and get their reaction. *Not one objected.* We had successfully overcome their fears. Our proposal went forward and finally—after years of unsuccessful attempts to link the original central business district with the developing highway business district—it was done.

Now, years later, one property has been redeveloped with retail, another is the site of a bank, and a third is still doing just fine in its original use. More important, new investment in the "triangle" has drawn the elements of community together much better than the status quo could ever have done.

The two keys to success were:

Don't limit your options to the way it's always been done. We reasoned that if we could create non-conforming uses, then we could make the rules to enable whatever we needed to make it work *and* acceptable to the affected parties.

Take the time and effort to talk to the people your proposal will impact the most. By going to them with both our dilemma and our proposal to make it work, we got their respect as well as their acceptance. They appreciated the extent to which we recognized their needs and were willing to incorporate them in our rezoning plan.

Off with His Head!

Critics of the Veterans Administration clamored for the firing of retired General Eric Shinseki over the revelations of massive failures in the VA hospital system. Traditionally this is the well-trodden path for political leaders and corporate boards to take when such incidents occur, especially on a national stage. Viewed dispassionately, however, how can a single individual rationally be responsible for a breakdown in a huge system? In local government it's easier to make a connection between leaders and the mistakes and argue that they should have addressed systemic failures. Embracing lean management might argue for setting a slightly higher tolerance bar for mistakes.

In 2008, John Shook, senior advisor of the Lean Enterprise Institute, described lean management: "Traditional management places tremendous pressure on individuals to be right....You must have a Solution, must know The Answer. Exposing problems, developing countermeasures, and learning from them doesn't just *support* lean management; it *is* lean management."

Should you fire a person who makes a mistake?

I suppose the correct answer is, "It depends." But I'm going to argue that exposing the mistake fits right into the lean management cycle and provides an opportunity. It's what you do about it that determines whether you're practicing what you preach. If you terminate the person—whether a leader or anyone else in the organization simply for a mistake—you send the message that innovation and its inherent risks are not worth taking. Early in my career the mayor of the city where I was city administrator said, "If you're not making a mistake then you're probably not doing anything." To him a communication failure was more damaging than a mistake. He applied the same principles in his own successful food processing business, implementing a forerunner of lean management long before the term entered our lexicon.

This viewpoint was recently reinforced in a *SmartBlog on Leadership* post by Jennifer Miller: "A leader with fortitude looks beyond the mistake and placing blame, to the bigger picture… so that all parties… learn and perhaps even come out stronger in the end."

Fixing the problems at the VA will take a lot more than new leadership. But the current crisis begs to be compared to many opportunities to exhibit "courageous leadership" at the local level.

Missing a Once-in-a-Lifetime Opportunity?

Historians are going to look back at this time in our nation's history and shake their heads at the missed opportunities cities, counties, states and school districts failed to capitalize on. With interest rates at the lowest we're likely to see in a lifetime, contractors hungry and willing to bid competitively, and people who need work, we're in a position to "kill a lot of birds with the same stone" and our slingshots are empty.

Local bond issues, borrowing to finance local and state capital construction projects, have been a time honored way to finance the building of facilities vital to the service of our communities. However, this avenue is being ignored at a time when water and sewer systems, roads, bridges, schools—all of the very things that we've been told over and over again are falling apart—could be built, repaired, or expanded to keep America competitive for generations to come.

With every bond issue there's someone who looks forward and calculates the payments on principal and interest and complains about how much the project is going to cost by the time the last payment is made. Well guess what, these needs aren't going to go away and interest rates aren't going to stay this low forever. We're at a point where we're just about as close as we're ever likely to come to being able to use "free money". There used to be an advertising campaign for a brand of automotive oil filter with the tag line "You can pay me now or pay me later." Maybe that should be our national motto. If we wait around much longer fearing anti-tax movements instead of jumping on this once in a lifetime chance, we'll be sorry. The work we'll need to do to stay on top in this world will cost more, if we can even afford to do it, and America's leading position will be that much harder to maintain.

I don't want to be able to say "I told you so."

Everyone Is Driving a "Used" Car

One response to the rapid and severe reduction in revenue experienced by many jurisdictions has been to delay capital expenditures such as vehicle replacement. While this may be an effective short-term strategy, occasionally replacement is the only option. However, the high cost of replacing old vehicles or equipment may be mitigated by buying used rather than new.

Many agencies in Washington purchase used vehicles and equipment through the state surplus program. Depending on your needs and the state's inventory, sometimes buying on the open market may be cheaper. Auctions, for example, offer an option.

Washington state law, RCW 39.30.045, authorizes municipalities to purchase goods through "... auctions conducted by the U.S. government or any agency thereof, any agency of the state of Washington, any municipality or other government agency, or any private party without being subject to public bidding requirements if those items can be obtained at a competitive price." Similar authorization undoubtedly exists for public agencies in other states.

This is elaborated on in MRSC publications *The Bidding Book for Washington Cities and Towns* and *The Bidding Book for Washington Counties*: "Sometimes a city will find exactly what it needs, at a favorable price, at an auction…This authority, it would seem, would allow a city to make a purchase on an internet-based auction service, such as E-bay, as well as through more traditional, in-person auctions."

Over the years the threshold for requiring competitive bids has remained at a level that makes it possible to buy a piece of used equipment or a vehicle and stay below the $7,500 limit (applicable to code cities under 20,000 population, towns, and second-class cities) without calling for bids.

It is also possible that purchase of a used vehicle may qualify for the "special market condition" that would allow bid law to be waived. If this exemption is used, the agency should document (preferably by resolution) the facts of the purchase, why the particular vehicle is available, and that the cost is less than the lowest list price otherwise available to the city.

There may be times when it is advantageous to call for bids, however. When buying used items you can write detailed specifications. That provides flexibility in your call for bids, thus allowing your agency to get the most for its dollar.

Several years ago rental car companies offered seminars on writing specifications for bids on used cars and trucks to encourage the resale of their fleets. Perhaps the strength of the economy in the years since then has made this a lost art, but it is still possible and MRSC has had inquiries from agencies interested in buying used vehicles again.

As a city administrator, I supervised the purchase of used vehicles through various means. When writing specifications, we would include a range of acceptable models, years, mileage, and equipment. Then we included an important key phrase: *"The city reserves the right to inspect and select the vehicle(s) with the combination of age, mileage, equipment and condition best suited to the city's needs."*

This gave us the essential discretion to select from "apples and oranges" when looking at various similar (but not exactly the same) vehicles. Using this process, we made many successful purchases while saving thousands of dollars.

Reconditioning Existing Fleet Vehicles May Also Be Worth Considering

An alternative to buying a used vehicle is to recondition what you already own. Traditionally the trucking industry has done this by installing "gliders," essentially entirely new frame and drive trains under a heavy truck tractor. Certain types of public vehicles with similar characteristics can be given many more years of service life this way.

On one occasion, we were considering replacing a major piece of fire apparatus. Units just like it were still being produced so we contacted the manufacturer for a proposal to recondition our truck to "like new" condition. We saved tens of thousands of dollars over the price of a new replacement. It's reasonable to consider doing the same with other vehicles.

We also tried this once with police patrol cars. We had some cars that officers liked but were no longer in production. For each car we had the suspension rebuilt and the drive train (engine and transmission) replaced with new factory units. The cars were back in service for much less than replacements would have cost.

There are some potential downsides to purchasing used vehicles. One issue related several years ago by a California fleet manager was that employees tended to be less tolerant with breakdowns of used vehicles. He said that a major mechanical issue with a new vehicle would be almost taken in stride by employees, while a relatively minor issue with a used car would be seen as the fault of it being a used car. A second consideration is that they are "used." When buying them for your agency, consider that you may have to, and should, spend the time and money to thoroughly service the vehicle. This will not only help ensure a longer service life but also go a long way toward avoiding the criticism described by the California manager.

In addition to the refurbished public safety vehicles I described, examples from my own experience of the type of successful used vehicle purchases include right-hand-drive vehicles from the Postal Service for meter reading, Jeep Cherokees from state surplus for building inspectors, light-duty trucks from dealers and private parties, heavy-duty trucks from both public and private sources, and cars from various sources. Only one car turned out to be a "lemon." Many returned years of service in their "second life" with the city saving thousands of dollars in the bargain.

Managing with Compassion

You can develop your management *skills* through education, training and experience. But you develop your management *style* through your innate personality and fundamental values. I've concluded that compassion is an integral part of my management style. It has contributed to my stock of experiences—both good and bad.

One of my staff members suffered some personal reversals that left him and his two sons temporarily homeless. Once that crisis passed, he got involved in a self-help housing program that required a commitment of several hundred hours to build the group of houses for program participants. No one could occupy their own house until all the houses were completed. Since he had quite a bit of leave on the books, he approached me about using one day a week for up to a year to fulfill his commitment. We had no policy in place for such a request. In addition, with his responsibilities a reduction in his work week to 32 hours might place a burden on the city. Yet I approved his request on the spot and I'd do it again. It turned out to pose no problems for the city at all, and it proved to be a genuine turning point in his life. He went on to serve on the board of directors of that housing program, helping many more people attain home ownership. He remained with the city and retired after many more very productive years of public service.

On another occasion, a key employee suffered a stroke that initially appeared to be career-ending. To everyone's relief he regained his speech and mobility and returned to work. I believed that would be the end of the story. Unfortunately, I soon began hearing rumors that his decision-making skills had suffered as a result of the stroke. I confirmed that the rumors were true, so he couldn't continue in his present position. However, he was only months away from qualifying for a pension and Social Security benefits.

One of his skills, completely apart from his official duties, was cabinetry. That skill hadn't been affected. So when I met with him to explain that he could not remain in his present job, I made him an offer: we would appoint him as our official furniture maker until he met the minimum retirement age, mere months away. He was to make any and all tables, cabinets, lockers, shelves, and similar furniture the city needed. We would supply the materials. He was very appreciative of the offer and I have no doubt that many items he made are still in use. In retrospect, I probably should have investigated his eligibility for disability payments. But simply arranging a change of assignment allowed him to be productive and gave him an opportunity to excel.

At the other end of the spectrum are a few incidents I'd like to forget, when my sense of compassion clouded my better judgment.

As I listened to an employee's tearful explanation of the circumstances leading to her disciplinary action, I accepted her account of events and did not end her employment. But a few months later I uncovered another clear instance of her wrongdoing and discharged her after all. Perhaps taking a harder line in the first instance would have spared me some grief later on.

Another instance involved an employee who seemed to be top notch. He was well-qualified for his position, even overqualified. But he was found to be deliberately shirking some responsibilities during unsupervised shifts. Public health was at risk. With no previous history of poor behavior and an outstanding technical background, I considered this incident as a "first offense" in applying disciplinary action. With the benefit of hindsight, that was a mistake. Although his return to work following a brief suspension included an agreement to work for the good of the organization, I'm convinced that a whole series of problems ensuing in that department, and beyond, stemmed directly from his position.

One time I was presented with two candidates for a promotion. On paper, one of them seemed more qualified. But I had serious doubts about his interpersonal skills, which I thought were important in the position. I promoted the other person instead. The unsuccessful candidate met with me and presented a well-worn letter of resignation describing all the issues he believed were plaguing his department. Part of the letter discussed in detail an incident when he claimed to have stepped in to pacify a citizen who had been treated rudely by his coworker—the one I had promoted. Unbeknownst to him, I knew the citizen and the incident. The roles had been the *exact opposite* of what this disgruntled employee recounted. *He* had been the rude one and his coworker had been the peacemaker. In many of the other assertions, he viewed the use of discretion as evidence of wrongdoing rather than a legitimate exercise in judgment. Knowing of his quality resume, I urged him to reconsider resigning and think about it over the weekend. I later learned that during our meeting and a follow-up before he left our employment he had been armed with a small handgun. Had I literally dodged a bullet?

A public sector manager often must manage sensitive personnel situations in the public eye. Decisions may be dissected and editorialized. In a unionized workforce they may be made even more difficult by contracts, laws, and third party arbitrators. In hiring, you need to be observant of characteristics that may develop into problems later. In discipline, you must follow the prescribed processes carefully but respectfully.

My management experiences have been predominantly positive. When I put them all into perspective, the good outweighed the bad by far.

All things considered, I would have preferred to avoid the consequences of having placed more trust in a few employees than they deserved. Placing trust and respect at the forefront makes the supervision of such people very difficult and may occasionally put one at a disadvantage. Fortunately, I could count such encounters in my career on the fingers of one hand. Conversely, I have no way to know how many other people's lives I positively affected when I erred on the side of compassion. I do know that even some employees who I was forced to discharge or discipline let it be known that they appreciated being treated with dignity and respect.

I wouldn't have it any other way.

Do Public Employees Lose Their Freedom of Speech?

I suspect that every local government executive has experienced the situation in which an employee unexpectedly steps to the microphone during a public comment period about a government issue or gets a letter published in a local newspaper. Before you hear or read the first word, you suppress your initial reaction and mentally prepare yourself for whatever comes next. In any organization there will be enough diversity that employees are bound to have differing opinions on matters of policy. In our society, where freedom of speech is a fundamental constitutional right, there will be times when public employment and public policy debates intersect. But critics may argue that the employee was prompted to speak out by their supervisor as a way of influencing the policymakers outside their official role in the process. This perception can be dangerous to a public manager's career and, if true, a likely violation of the Code of Ethics for International City/County Management Association (ICMA) members.

So What Is a Public Executive to Do?

Can, or should, you prevent an employee from speaking out on issues or take any action against an employee in such a situation?

A century or more ago, the Supreme Court would likely have upheld the right of a public employer to discharge an employee for advocating for or against an issue before the policymakers. Justice Oliver Wendell Holmes wrote in 1892, "There may be a constitutional right to talk politics, but there is no constitutional right to be a policeman." This position lasted until the late 1960s, when the Court rejected the notion and began to apply a balancing test between the employee's right to free expression and the public entity's need to maintain an efficient workplace.

Under the balancing test employed by the Court in *Pickering v. Board of Education,* 391 U.S. 563 (1968), to determine whether a public employer's discipline of an employee that is related to his/her speech violated the First Amendment, it must first be demonstrated that the employee is addressing a matter of public concern and not something solely related to the employee's own personal situation.

Once the subject matter of the speech is determined to be of public concern, the courts will then balance whether the employee's free-speech interest outweighs the employer's interest in maintaining an efficient workplace. In doing so, the courts generally consider whether the employee's speech:

· Impairs discipline or harmony among co-workers.

· Has a detrimental impact on close working relationships for which personal loyalty and confidence are necessary.

· Interferes with the normal operation of the employer's business.

Generally, the higher up the ladder the employee is in the organization, the more likely his or her speech will have an impact on the second phase of the test. Supervisory employees are, by definition, responsible for maintaining discipline, close working relationships, and smooth operations. Therefore, a derogatory or disruptive opinion expressed by a person in such a position may fail the second part of the test and not be considered protected speech.

To Answer the Question I Posed Earlier: What Should You Do?

If rank and file employees attend a council meeting and complain about a policy issue, it's likely well within their right to do so under the First Amendment. It's also unlikely you'll hear about it until it happens and equally unlikely that you'll be blamed if they do. On the other hand, when a mid-level manager or a department head decides to take issue with the council or board and goes to the media or takes the microphone at a public meeting, chances are you'll have an inkling it is on the way. If you have the opportunity, you may be able to discuss with the employee the implications of "speaking their mind" on the subject and let them decide if they should proceed. You may also be able to prepare the policymakers by advising them that some staff members have strong opinions and that they are likely to hear from them. In such an instance it may also be possible to compile the comments and concerns of staff members anonymously to provide the decision-makers with those comments without jeopardizing either the employees' right of expression or their employment status.

This is not intended to be a legal opinion. Cases heard and decided by the Supreme Court since *Pickering* have added to case law. If you're faced with a situation where you believe it necessary to take disciplinary action, you should consult your agency's attorney and/or an employment law specialist.

The Paralysis of Analysis

"A good plan violently executed right now is far better than a perfect plan executed next week."

- George S. Patton

Clearly the General was talking about a battle plan, but I've heard this point paraphrased in regard to just about any activity. A lot of authors on a wide variety of topics agree with Patton.

Why? I'll call it "the perfection of information curve." As you begin to learn or gather information, the quantity and quality of what you learn rises rapidly at first. As time passes, the rate slows down and gradually the learning curve flattens out. Waiting longer yields only minimal improvements in the quality of the facts gathered.

There is an optimum point at which good information can be applied to yield a good decision, though the exact point isn't defined. As public officials, we're often faced with decisions that require us to obtain additional information from specialists. We depend on planners, engineers, public safety professionals, and others with specialized training and expertise to give us the background we need so we can decide and move on. Unfortunately, too often the public sector is plagued with the "paralysis of analysis," so much so that it has become a punch line. Regrettably, this is somewhat understandable, given the competing interests that frequently want diametrically opposing outcomes. It's often easier to order another study than to make a decision. That's the time to remember the General's words and ask: Will the value added by further study yield an improvement in the final decision that is equal to or greater than the cost of the delay or simply even the cost of the study itself?

Sometimes this is easy. You know intuitively when you've got a clear picture of the facts and an answer seems obvious. In other instances, one or more interest groups is urging more study or advocating a completely contrary decision.

Is this a legitimate policy choice or merely a delaying tactic? As I said, the optimum point isn't predetermined. Your relationship with, and confidence in, those who advise you, as well as your own experience, are what you have to rely upon. Consider all the information you've received. Then decide if you have gathered what you need or if you have not yet reached the decision point. But do whatever you can to avoid the "paralysis of analysis."

Getting What You Want through Foresight and Creativity: Part 4

Art, Antiques and Easements—Is This City Hall or Antiques Roadshow?

What the Heck is an "Art Easement" Anyway?

Many communities have a public art program that sets aside a small portion of public projects for the installation of works of art. In many cases the works are incorporated into the structure or landscaping, or displayed in the project itself to enhance its attractiveness. Sometimes, though, a project doesn't lend itself to the inclusion of art and the funds are set aside for something that can be displayed where it will have better exposure. Such was the case in our community, when funds were available at the time a significant expansion of the library was being planned.

As the project progressed, the architect worked with the public art committee on possible locations for works that could be incorporated into the building. They selected a few prominent locations and began the process of soliciting proposals from well-qualified artists. The committee made a final selection and it looked like everything was going fine.

Until . . . someone realized that we couldn't spend public money for the art. Like many cities, we were part of a library district. This district provided the actual services but the building belonged to a private non-profit group. While its purpose was to own the structure and grounds, the fact that it was not public property precluded installing public art that would essentially become part of the building.

We called a meeting of the interested parties to consider the situation. The library district was eager to expand its services and didn't want to delay the construction. The group that owned the building wanted the art works to enhance the building. But they didn't want to turn the building over to a public agency, particularly after an extensive private fundraising campaign to finance the expansion. The public art committee saw it as a perfectly appropriate place to display the works they'd commissioned and just wanted the matter resolved. No one seemed to have any ideas that would enable things to move forward.

Since the construction was, in reality, a private project, the city had not been directly involved. Although the public art committee worked with city funds, they functioned relatively independently. So we had no idea that they had been working toward including public art in the project.

Attending this meeting was my first direct involvement. My first reaction was that it would not be possible to do the proposed installation. Perhaps pieces of art could be on display but a permanent installation would be impossible. Public money simply could not be spent on private property.

As I listened to everyone, it occurred to me that public utilities are installed on private property all the time when property owners grant an easement on the property. I suggested that the property owner could grant an "art easement" to the city. That would allow the placement of the art, much the same as a property owner would grant an easement to install a public water line on their property. The art would remain the property of the city and—just like a utility line—the city would retain the right to inspect and maintain it as needed. Everyone agreed that it might just work and I had the city attorney review the idea and draft the necessary document.

It may be the only one of its kind but our art easement was quickly prepared and ratified by all parties, thereby allowing the inclusion of public art in the new library.

The easement not only dealt with the initial problem of installing the art works on private property, it has the added benefit of clarifying ownership and responsibilities without relying on oral understandings and people's memories. This is especially important for a facility that will likely remain in service long after the people who made the agreement are gone.

Model Ts and Volunteers

Our city had a long history of service from its volunteer fire department. One symbol of that history was a Ford Model T fire truck reputed to have been the first piece of motorized fire apparatus in the county, predating even the first fire trucks in the region's largest city. It sat proudly in a place of honor in the main station and was always a feature in local parades. According to the fire chief, there were many purchase offers for it from collectors and museums. But no one wanted to risk losing it. I was also told that it "belonged" to the volunteers. The city had given it to them long ago.

The years had taken their toll. Several lumpy coats of brush-applied red paint only looked good from about fifty feet away. As the community approached the 100th anniversary of its founding, the volunteers wanted to undertake a thorough restoration. One of them owned a body shop and agreed to lead the project. The truck was completely torn apart. The paint was stripped, metal repaired, wood replaced, brass polished, and the whole truck treated to the latest technology paint with gold pin striping. All the work was done by the dedicated volunteer firefighters themselves.

After all that effort I wanted to assure that it was protected. I began a search through the city records to find out what conditions, if any, had been stipulated when the city transferred the truck to the volunteers. I could find no record that the truck had been transferred. In fact, the title was still in the city's name and the city had been routinely insuring it for years.

No one, including me, had any intention of altering the "understanding" that the truck belonged to the volunteers. Yet something had to be done to establish a proper record. I proposed a new written agreement between the volunteer firefighters association and the city. The volunteers met my proposal with more than a little suspicion, thinking perhaps the city wanted to reclaim the truck after all their work.

The chief and I brought the truck to city hall the night the new agreement was on the agenda so the city council could see the finished project. The council passed a resolution formally transferring the truck to the volunteers in recognition of their service to the community and their beautiful restoration job. The volunteers were pleasantly surprised (and probably relieved) by the recognition they received. Coupled with the council resolution was a written agreement stipulating in more detail the terms and conditions. It also required that the vehicle remain in the community and revert to the city if the volunteers association ceased to exist.

Now there is a written record of the transfer of the antique vehicle that should outlive the people involved, just as the vehicle itself has lasted far beyond the lives of the first volunteers who served with it. As with the art easement, creating a written record of the city council's action is intended to prevent future disputes over the disposition of the vehicle if or when the question ever arises.

Monday, Monday

The Mamas and the Papas and the Carpenters lamented the opening day of the work week lyrically. Their sentiments no doubt contributed to the motive for moving several of the federal holidays to Mondays.

Every few years, in addition to those federal Monday holidays, several "date-specific" holidays fall on Mondays too. It reminds me of an unsuccessful attempt to change a city policy on solid waste collection, which demonstrated the lessons to be learned from failure.

Our city collected solid waste with a hardworking and dedicated crew of workers who performed well in all kinds of weather, but dealing with holidays was always difficult. On the day after the holiday, they had two routes to cover. Even though we paid overtime if necessary and could supplement the crew with other staff and backup equipment, it was always grueling and hard on morale.

Our supervisor of utilities recommended that we stop trying to catch up on the day after the holiday by just skipping the route that fell on the holiday and collecting the trash on the regular schedule the following week. Customers on the affected routes could set out twice the normal volume of trash at no additional charge. We reasoned that we actually might collect less as customers might try to reduce their waste generation to get by for two weeks. We recommended it to the City Council and easily got their approval.

Prior to implementation we conducted a public information campaign by including notices with our utility bills. We promoted the change prominently in the local newspaper with official notices, a press release, and advertisements. There was little negative reaction.

We did *not* consult the calendar.

As it happened, the first year of implementation was on the calendar cycle when virtually every holiday in fell on a Monday. The same neighborhoods bore all of the effects of the new policy almost once a month.

Every community has a few active, articulate, and vocal citizens. Several of ours lived on the Monday collection route. When they realized the full implications of the revised collection policy, they wasted no time in lobbying the Mayor and City Council to abandon the new schedule. We tried to maintain that the one-week delay in service would eventually be rotated throughout the community, but to no avail. The fact that there would always be at least four Monday holidays every year kept the opposition alive and stopped the idea for good.

Any new proposal can be defeated by failing to consider all the potential impacts. Something as simple as consulting the calendar prior to implementation might have alerted us to the fact that one route would bear the brunt of the inconvenience by starting when we did. Delaying the start of the new schedule until mid-year would have effectively delayed the impact on the Monday collection route by several years, perhaps even allowing the new policy to gain acceptance by then.

We'll never know.

Don't Ask

A recent post on the *Today* show website by author Eve Tahmincioglu discussing whether certain questions in employment interviews were illegal reminded me of my own experience in representing the city in an official inquiry into a hiring decision.

Seeking to fill a meter-reading position, our public works department advertised for the opening, stressing the need for attention to detail. One applicant, who was not a finalist for the position, had written "I am a ***** - American," indicating his ethnic background, in the margin of the application. Nowhere on the application was there a question asking for this information.

He filed a discrimination complaint with the Washington State Human Rights Commission. I represented the city at the initial meeting with the investigator. I was pretty confident in the appropriateness of our hiring decision but never the less apprehensive about my first experience in responding to a discrimination complaint.

In preparation, I reviewed the details of the hiring with the public works supervisor, including a review of the applications from both the person hired and the complainant. The successful candidate had experience in inventory control with a major manufacturer and had submitted a neat and concise application and resume. The unsuccessful applicant's application was not very neat, and his resume had inconsistent employment dates, apparent gaps and overlaps in employment, and no experience particularly relevant to meter reading. Given the necessity for a meter reader to work independently and accurately with great attention to detail, I too would have selected the one with the background in inventory control and the clear, concise resume over the complainant.

The complainant and I met with the investigator. He stated that he believed he'd been discriminated against because of his ethnic background as written on his application and basically left it at that. I responded that we hadn't asked for ethnic background information and that, given the requirements for meter reading accuracy, his application did not make a very good case, especially in comparison to the successful candidate. I had copies with me for illustration.

After a few more questions from the investigator, the complainant was asked to leave. I expected a lecture or something but to my surprise the investigator told me she thought the city was being "set up" by this fellow and that he might try to apply again. She recommended closing the case with a finding of "no reasonable cause."

Within weeks we had an opening at the municipal cemetery. Sure enough, the same man applied. The cemetery manager interviewed all the applicants and this man assured him he had lots of experience in using maintenance equipment— in particular a backhoe, an absolute necessity in excavating for burials. Excavations are frequently in tight spaces with well-tended landscaping, fragile monuments, and previously interred remains close by. The manager had devised a test to gauge a worker's skill in digging precisely and neatly with the backhoe by outlining the size of a typical grave plot with string and asking each applicant to dig within the lines. He explained the test to each finalist (including our suspected fraudster) and set up an appointment for each of them to show what they could do.

We never heard from that guy again.

What did we learn from this experience? Make sure your application and interview processes are relevant to the job. This reminder shouldn't be necessary but as the Today.com article points out, some areas are "murky." Though the state has its own laws in addition to federal law, it pays to err on the side of caution. Stay away from questions or skill tests that aren't job-related. Avoid murkiness. MRSC has abundant resource materials on human resource practices and the laws on discrimination to help you to make a fair (and legal) assessment of candidates.

Finally, just because someone asserts that you've unlawfully discriminated, *don't panic*. Review what you've done and prepare a clear, concise explanation for the preliminary investigation. You may have legal counsel if you wish but it may not be necessary, as I learned.

Major Public Project
Information/Participation Process

Perhaps no municipal project is more fraught with danger than undertaking a major street or utility reconstruction project through the middle of your central business district. There are the obvious dangers associated with working around aging, fragile infrastructure that can create nasty surprises—flood, fire, famine. (Famine? Ever have to shut off the water to your central business district just as the lunch rush began?) Just as hazardous are the public relations pitfalls that can doom a career overnight.

Here are some tips and strategies that can help you survive, gleaned from a career that included receiving our state Mainstreet Association's "Outstanding Public Partner" award by the local downtown association for successfully working with them on a major project.

Even before the final go/no-go decision on the project has been made, start preparing the information and communication plan you'll need once it is definitely moving forward. We often focus on the physical and fiscal aspects of the project—design, bidding, contracting and construction—and regard the less tangible parts like public information almost as a nuisance. This can be a career-ending underestimation. Keeping project supporters, beneficiaries, critics, and observers well-informed about its status and impact on them can have tremendous positive impact on the public's perception of not only the project but also your staff, your agency—and you.

Identify Any Public Concerns ASAP!

Whether through brainstorming with staff and elected officials or an advisory group, you should identify potential issues that may arise as a result of project construction.

> - Businesses – What impacts will there be on parking and store access from noise, dust, traffic disruption/detours, deliveries, utility interruptions, etc.?

> - Residents – Are there residents in the area? The same issues affect them.

> - Commuters – Do commuters regularly traverse the area? Parking availability and detours can affect their travel times and what they might do in the area while going to and from work.

- Visitors – Is tourism a significant contributor to the local economy? How will you communicate important project information to them? What can you do to avoid permanent damage to that part of the economy and minimize the temporary disruption?

Hold Public Meetings, Open Houses

Include your public information process in the project design meetings. As they say in public speaking: Tell them what you're going to say, say what you're going to say, and then tell them what you said. While you're explaining the details of the project, let your audience know how you'll be keeping them informed as the project moves forward so they'll know what to look for. If you can create a theme or catchphrase for the project, do it. Treat it like an advertising campaign. It benefits your project by making your information identifiable and it helps link announcements to the business community, giving them the opportunity to build advertising aimed at keeping customers while it may be a bit more inconvenient to get there. Part of what earned our city's "Outstanding Public Partner" recognition was an advertising campaign with a clever catchphrase that provided important public access and detour information along with promotion for the impacted businesses.

Establish Rapport/Dialogue

You should be open to the affected residents and property owners. Generate lists for paper or electronic communication from the meetings and open houses. This can be a good opportunity to use a social network like Twitter for a personal project update to subscribers. Old-fashioned personal one-on-one communication may be slow but it's effective.

Consider an Advisory Committee

You only have so many hours in the day, and most likely a limited staff to work with. An advisory committee can be an effective multiplier. Periodic meetings with a representative committee comprised of affected residents, owners and other stakeholders can alert you to issues that may be brewing before they boil over in a public hearing or letter to the editor. They also give you the opportunity to have more "in depth" conversations regarding the project with people in a position to carry the message much better than what you might be able to get out in a short sound bite or quote in typical media coverage.

After the meeting you can send meeting notes annotated with further explanations and/ action items. It also provides an opportunity to coordinate with other departments, agencies and elected officials (schools, parks, fire, DOT, and local or regional transit).

Involve
Your communication list should include:

Property owners

Residents

Neighbors

The Chamber of Commerce

The downtown association or retail trade group

Advisory committee (if any)

Schools

Transit

DOT, state/county as appropriate

Detours and Traffic
Involve/notify the same groups

Lynn Nordby

Communication Plan

Do one!

Don't be afraid to overdo it!

Not less than one month ahead: large signs, on- site information boards/kiosks

Not less than 3 weeks ahead: Mail flyers to a wide list—include overview, detailed detour information and ask for cooperation and patience. Include suggestions on how to cope (carpool, telecommuting, allow more time, combine trips, alternate work schedules, etc.)

Press releases: Send to newspapers, radio and television about 3 weeks before the start

About 2 weeks ahead: press conference, press release

Use web site, project hotline, consider traffic cams linked to website, social network sites, blog, listserv email service daily update to interested parties

On the project start day have plenty of flaggers and extra police officers on hand, make sure they're well-briefed and have something printed to hand out

Consider a "table tent" or flyer (daily, weekly, or whatever is appropriate) update for restaurant tables in the affected area

Provide regular status reports to property owners, use advisory committee or public meetings to determine desired/optimal frequency

Consider working with your downtown association or Chamber of Commerce on an ad campaign providing useful project information in combination with promotion for the impacted businesses.

Recycled Railroad Right-of-Way

Sometimes a potential asset is right in front of you but it takes patience, persistence, and perseverance to take advantage of it. When I heard that the railroad was going to abandon its right-of-way through our city, my initial concern was securing the grade crossings for our existing streets and hopefully acquiring one or two more to improve the traffic circulation in our central business district. In addition, our chamber of commerce had been leasing a couple of public parking areas for the CBD on the edge of the right-of-way and we hoped to permanently acquire those too.

I drafted a letter to the railroad company . . . and waited . . . and waited . . . and waited. Finally, nearly a year later, I got a reply indicating that the company was interested in working with us but didn't know just what they actually owned. Maybe they owned it outright, like any other property owner. Or maybe they just had permission to use it, like an easement. The facts were shrouded in the mists of time (and two or three mergers and acquisitions in the last century or so).

The city attorney and I met with railroad executives and learned there were a couple of avenues toward clarifying ownership. We could seek a determination through Congress, or through a "court of competent jurisdiction." Without getting into politics I'll just say that our state senators advised us to stay away from Washington, D.C. lest the current administration try to take the property away from us altogether. Left with the judicial option, we devised an agreement with the railroad to embark on a lawsuit to "quiet title" to the property, thereby establishing firmly who owned it and just what their interest was. The agreement needed approval from various offices of the railroad so it was duly sent on its rounds and again we waited . . . and waited . . . and waited. Railroad bureaucracy seemed to make any other organizational bureaucracy pale in comparison. Nearly another year passed before we were contacted by the regional property managers and asked to meet again.

Much to our surprise we were informed that as the agreement made its rounds, the railroad had determined that our right-of-way was part of what they called "Act of Congress" right-of-way. During the Civil War, Congress granted the railroad companies outright ownership of alternating sections (a square mile) of land in a checkerboard pattern in the western states to promote railway expansion and development in the West. In the sections they weren't given outright, they were granted ownership of a strip 400 feet wide at the time they laid track. Furthermore, federal law stipulated that if right-of-way was within the city limits at the time of abandonment, ownership would revert to the city.

The only hurdle left to clear was how to deal with the property in the marketplace. Historically railroad right-of-way was acquired by so many varied means that ownership was usually clouded. Since we hadn't pursued the judicial option, all we really had was the railroad's word for it. Any decision to sell, trade, or lease the property would need title insurance. Preliminary inquiries to the title insurance industry were met with a cold shoulder. They weren't interested. Title searches for railroad property were just too much work, they said.

Undaunted, we learned that the present-day Bureau of Land Management maintains the records of land transfers dating back to the origins of the Homestead Act and the beginning of western settlement. If we could determine that the railroad was there before any settlers, we could prove an unbroken line of ownership from the United States government to the railroad company to the city. Fortunately, our search of photocopies of the handwritten records from BLM proved that the railroad arrived just prior to the first recorded deeds of the town's first settlers and land developers. Now that *we* had done the work, the title companies were only too happy sell us a title insurance policy for the property.

With the help of a citizens' task force, the city council adopted a master plan with the goal of maintaining the property primarily in public ownership, opening new street access, and making sites available for essential public facilities.

Today the former right-of-way has provided sites for a public library, a public works maintenance facility, parks, trails, post office facilities, public parking, a motel with a restaurant, and a small Sears store. One land swap secured convenient public parking for downtown but the balance remains in public ownership.

The final result far exceeded our modest initial hopes for the disposition of the surplus railroad property, and long-term benefits are still accruing to the community.

Saving the $12,000 Closet

During my career I've been responsible for millions of dollars of municipal facilities construction above and below ground. City halls, public works yards, reservoirs, sewage treatment plants, utility lines of all kinds, streets, sidewalks, and parking lots were some of the more significant projects.

In the course of these capital improvements, I gained knowledge and learned lessons that improved how I managed each succeeding project. I enjoy learning how things work. Understanding the interrelatedness of a project's parts has proven invaluable.

As a manager, whether it's the construction of a utility line or a public building, you must maintain an overall view of the entire project even though the details may be intriguing and constantly draw you closer. But even when we have highly trained professionals at our disposal, too much attention to the details can obscure the "big picture" and sometimes lead to wasted resources, or embarrassment at the very least.

We were in the process of a total renovation of City Hall. The core of the building had been constructed in the early 1920s with additions and remodels in the succeeding seven decades. It was time for an "Extreme Makeover—City Hall Edition." Haphazard and poorly executed remodels needed to go. So did vestiges of functions no longer carried on in the building like the water reservoir telemetry, the volunteer firefighter call siren, and old jail cells, along with hazardous materials like asbestos. Given the attractive and historic nature of the exterior, we decided to try to make the new interior more traditional in appearance and yet functional with new technology and energy efficiency. We chose an excellent architect and got a good bid from a qualified contractor. In general the project progressed fairly smoothly, even the asbestos abatement.

Then I injured my back. The doctor ordered me to remain flat on my back. After about two weeks I didn't think I could take any more. The office called and asked if there was any way I could come to an urgent meeting with the contractor and the architect. Of course! I put on my back brace.

The architect proceeded with a presentation regarding the need for a significant change order to install a large steel beam to support the upper floor in place of a bearing wall.

Formerly an exterior wall in one of the building's earlier configurations, it had to be removed to enlarge one of the restrooms for handicapped access. This was going to be a major effort involving structural engineering to determine the appropriate size of the beam, additional demolition inside for columns to support the beam, the beam itself, and the labor to install it. In addition, it looked like significant changes to an adjacent room housing the new data and electrical panels for the building would be required.

I asked why this level of construction was necessary and was told that a brick wall on the second floor had to be supported by this beam when the wall below was removed to enlarge the restroom. As I looked at the preliminary drawings and asked a few more questions, I realized that the second floor wall they were trying to preserve was merely the exterior of an old stairwell that had been closed off and turned into a storage closet as part of a previous remodel.

This change order would have created a most expensive closet!

Everyone had become so fixated on solving the problem of supporting the wall on the upper floor that they lost sight of the "big picture." What purpose did the wall serve? Without hesitation I made the decision and told the architect and contractor to simply tear the "closet" off the building and close up the opening. There was no need for any of the proposed extra design work and construction. Instead of thousands of dollars to save the closet, only a few hundred extra in demolition was required.

As managers we're responsible for keeping our eyes on the overall goals of the organization as we deal with the everyday details.

So how can we avoid the pitfall of focusing too closely and losing sight of the goal?

Capital Projects

Make a conscious effort to understand and focus on the project as a whole rather than on the incremental steps. Even though we had an excellent core group of professionals with the city hall renovation, they became so involved in the immediate problem that they didn't realize that the actual use of the wall they were trying to preserve was unimportant.

Depending on the size of your organization, you may need to "wear more than one hat" and participate in detailed decision-making on a given project even though you may also have broader responsibilities for your agency. So before the project begins, familiarize yourself with its scope, budget, construction schedule, and sequence.

Look for points where the project may conflict with other projects and activities in the community such as fairs, festivals and seasonal events. Often the design and construction professionals may overlook a conflict, such as a major community event that will be disrupted by the project. Involving the Chamber of Commerce early in dealing with a downtown project is definitely superior to reacting to a conflict with an annual parade or street fair that your consulting engineer and the low bidder didn't know about and hadn't taken into account. On another project, we were able to avoid a major disruption of an annual street fair by working with the contractor to slightly delay the start of the project and extend the completion deadline so that street demolition could start after the event.

What is the project's relationship to the entire capital program for the year? Will it take more than a single budget/calendar year to complete? If so, budgeting and seasonal weather issues must also be taken into account.

Consider establishing an advisory committee. Even though it may seem like it's adding another layer to what might be an already complex project, a committee comprised of stakeholders—as well as some individuals who may not be directly affected by the project—can offer valuable perspective. Their ability to see your project from the outside can help you see things you might otherwise overlook or take for granted.

Policy or Planning Projects

Many plans we make in local government are easily compromised by daily incremental decisions that slowly begin to move us away from the vision that went into the initial long-range planning effort. The annual budgeting process is a short-to-intermediate-range plan that takes a large amount of time and effort. Budget decisions can support long-range plans or draw us away from them incrementally. Especially now that revenue shortfalls are requiring decisions on program reductions, it's hard to see beyond the moment. But now is also an opportunity to look ahead. Cuts made now may not be permanent. With a stabilized economy, with even modest growth, a future vision for your community is still attainable though the timeline or resources available will have to be adjusted. If you can, cut strategically so the core capacity of your organization isn't decimated. Think about institutional knowledge. Can you retain key employees with institutional memory?

Comprehensive Plans are typically broad in scope and long-range in nature. Frequently the ideals expressed in the comp plan are intended to be implemented through more detailed plan amendments, codes, and ordinances adopted subsequently that will specify the regulations necessary to fulfill the vision outlined in the original plan.

Given the time it takes and the occasional hurdles to move from the conceptual to the specific, months—even years—may pass between the time a comp plan is adopted and the preparation of the codes and ordinances needed to implement its policies. In the interval the makeup of the elected policymaking body can change. New members may not share the same assumptions as the group that adopted the original plan, or not having been part of the process they may be unaware of these assumptions.

Consider maintaining a chronology as the process moves along that documents the decisions and policies that have been adopted and why. This helps to keep the implementation regulations adopted later in perspective and reinforces the broader policies expressed at the start.

Keep the "big picture" in mind. With the City Hall renovation I was lucky. If I'd followed the doctor's orders and stayed in bed the closet might have been "saved." I was happy for an excuse to get out of the house and really happy I wasn't going to have to publicly explain why we'd spent thousands of dollars just to save a closet.

A Bond Issue Obstacle Course

After several years of effort, the city had at last secured ownership of a swath of abandoned railroad right-of-way through the heart of town. An extensive planning process involving a "blue ribbon" advisory committee had resulted in a master plan unanimously adopted by the city council. One of the cornerstones was a new library to replace the cramped and obsolete structure built several decades before.

Everything seemed in place for a beautiful civic project to serve as an anchor and demonstrate long-term commitment to our downtown. The library board of trustees and the friends of the library group asked the city council to submit a proposal to the voters for a bond issue to build the new facility. The city council authorized the selection of an architect to prepare a preliminary design and cost estimate before the ballot measure was submitted.

But no one anticipated the obstacles we would face.

Obstacle Number 1 – Historic Deed Restriction

Just as the project was about to be launched, a descendent of one of the community's earliest families informed the city council that the existing library property included a deed restriction requiring that it always be used as the library site. One of the founding families had donated their Victorian house and personal book collection as the town's first library with that restriction in place. The council was informed that any new facility had to be built right there.

Everything stopped while this claim was examined. If true, the city attorney advised us, the restriction could be removed but it would take time and money. Some people argued that the city would be doing a disservice to the memory of the original donors by breaking this apparently long-forgotten commitment.

With minimal effort we found that when the existing facility had been built, the city had discovered the deed restriction and contacted the heirs of the original donors to have it released.

Obstacle Number 2 – Architect Selection

A committee of library board members asked me to participate in the selection process along with the library director. After interviewing several architectural firms, the board made a selection and told the library director to negotiate a contract. Weeks passed because the director couldn't get a proposal from the firm. After consulting with me, he reached an agreement with the board's alternate choice.

Obstacle Number 3 – Location, Location, Location
Even though the city council had unanimously adopted the master plan, one or two councilmembers began having second thoughts about locating the library on the proposed site. Their reasoning seemed to be that the location might be better used for a revenue-generating commercial structure such as a fast-food franchise. Ultimately the council voted to proceed as planned but it wasn't unanimous, planting the seeds of the fourth obstacle.

Obstacle Number 4 – Election Number 1
The bond issue proposition was finally placed on the ballot. There was no organized opposition, although we heard comments that the positioning of the building—as illustrated by the simple schematic sketches in the master plan—would have "children running right into the street." Proponents tried to explain that these were not the actual design documents and that the final version would assure the safety of library patrons of any age. It wasn't enough. By a narrow margin the bond issue failed to get the needed 60%.

Obstacle Number 5 – Public Opinion Survey

The friends of the library were not deterred. They asked the city council for permission to use some of their donated funds to conduct a professional survey of voters' opinions about the library proposal. Those results indicated that uncertainty about the building's location on the property had been a factor. Had it been understood, the survey indicated the proposal would have gotten a 72% "Yes" vote!

Obstacle Number 6 – Election Number 2

Citing the survey, the friends of the library asked the city council to resubmit the issue to the voters.

While this was happening, a new law authorized "mail-only" ballots for special elections. In a couple of nearby municipal incorporation elections the propositions had passed with a mail-out ballot even though the same question had been rejected when placed on the general election ballot. Based on those successes and the survey, I recommended that the city council resubmit the issue to the voters using a mailed ballot.

The result: over 71% in favor! We authorized the architects to begin final design and bid documents.

Obstacle Number 7 – So Close, Yet so Far

While preparing for the actual bond issuance, our bond counsel prepared what is known as a transcript. This is a compilation of all the official documents necessary for the bond issue to take place, including the various resolutions and ordinances of the city council, official reports, the official statement from the city's financial advisors and, of course the election results including a copy of the official ballot from the county. The attorney discovered that the county had omitted the crucial ballot wording that the measure would authorize an "excess levy" to repay the bonds. Even though it would be hard to argue that anyone voting for the measure didn't understand that they were authorizing a tax increase, that's not what the ballot said. He could not give us the opinion that we were duly authorized to sell bonds and repay them with new tax dollars.

I was at a conference when I got the news. Stunned, I started home immediately. Passing through a town at lunchtime, I saw a sign that the local Rotary club was meeting that day. I decided to "kill two birds with one stone": have lunch and make up a meeting. As visitors were introduced I discovered that the Chief Justice of the State Supreme Court was also making up a meeting. I stayed afterward to ask his unofficial opinion. I suppose I was compromising his ability to help us out if the issue ever reached the Supreme Court, but what the heck, I had to ask. He was as surprised as me and said he had never heard of such a thing before.

We hoped the preponderance of evidence we had supporting our argument that the whole community understood the issue would be sufficient for us to proceed. Unfortunately we learned that a similar matter had been litigated in 1949 and the State Supreme Court had ruled that the wording on the ballot was binding. All design work was suspended while we regrouped.

Obstacle Number 8 – Election Number 3

By the time this problem was discovered, it was too late to put the issue on the primary election ballot. We had to wait for the next general election.

While there were a few rumblings in the community that the city must have made a mistake, all our documents were in order. The county admitted that the mistake was theirs. We asked that they mail a notice to all registered voters stating that they had made the mistake and that, although the results showed that it had passed, the election would need to be run again. County officials countered that "the measure had not passed since it was invalid." Rather than fight over that question, we conceded and the county mailed a notice explaining that they had mistakenly omitted the words authorizing an excess levy but not mentioning the results of the prior election. It was a small victory.

A long time had passed since the first steps toward this project had been taken. Inflation was a serious factor, particularly in construction costs, but we chose to stay within our original estimates and agreed to scale back the project if it became necessary.

Early returns looked like a repeat of the first election but by the time every ballot was counted we just cleared the 60% threshold for an excess levy. Phew!

By the time the library was completed I had accepted a position in another city. The city council and library board graciously invited me back for the dedication to savor the satisfaction of crossing the finish line with them.

Lessons Learned
Perseverance and Patience – This project took much longer than anticipated and faced several unforeseen roadblocks. Staying with it rewarded us with the desired outcome. Remaining patient in the face of some of the claims tossed about helped demonstrate our commitment and kept us from

being distracted from the goal. It was also valuable to insist that the county directly acknowledge its mistake to every voter, not just in a press release. Given the close results of the third election, it may have made the difference.

Expect the Unexpected – I would be surprised if many public entities would do a title search on a piece of property occupied by a public facility for nearly a century before simply considering moving to another location. We were caught off-guard by the claim that we were barred from leaving the site of the first library, but our predecessors had foreseen that eventuality and cleared our way decades before. The county didn't ask us to proofread the ballot before the election. I doubt that this occurs anywhere and no one noticed the missing words. We don't know why the first-choice architectural firm was unresponsive but the alternate proved to be exceptional.

The Value of a Well-done Survey – We were very pleasantly surprised when the second election results so nearly matched the projections from the public opinion survey. In contrast, I've seen several supposedly professional surveys with vague questions that yield meaningless results.

Don't Take Support for Granted – In spite of the unanimous vote adopting our master plan for the property, when the time came for a concrete proposal some policymakers had second thoughts. They're entitled to change their minds but we weren't aware that that had happened. In retrospect had we been able to address some of their concerns before putting the first proposal on the ballot we might have succeeded.

Many public projects face obstacles on the road from conception to realization. Keeping a clear focus on the finish line kept us from being overwhelmed or distracted by the eight obstacles we faced in completing our new library building.

Killing "Zombies"

A recent article from the blog of the Lincoln Institute of Land Policy introduced me to a new expression, "zombie subdivisions": residential developments approved on paper or partially complete, unoccupied, and requiring ongoing maintenance—without a corresponding contribution in taxes or utility charges. This reminded me of how through "foresight and creativity" we put a "zombie" to rest and preserved a valuable piece of recreational open space in a developing residential area.

Former military bases exist all over the country. Many have been returned to productive private use through creative and aggressive redevelopment projects. Some lie fallow, too remote, contaminated, or complicated to be economically viable, and some are like the zombie subdivisions described in the Lincoln Institute article. These properties were sold off long ago to developers and speculators during a previous economic bubble, then left dormant, undead, and ready to rise up and surprise an unsuspecting community.

In the 1890s the latest military technology was the battleship, which boasted large-diameter guns able to hurl explosive projectiles weighing hundreds or even thousands of pounds for miles at sea or land targets. Our nation built strategically located coastal artillery bases to protect important cities and military facilities from these behemoths. Several were located in the Pacific Northwest around Puget Sound. Like all military technology, something newer soon came along. The airplane quickly rendered these fixed installations obsolete.

After serving alternate purposes during the Second World War, many were declared surplus and sold off. Such was the case with one in our community. A portion of the property along the shoreline became a small state park, buildings were sold for residential use, and the open areas of the old post were subdivided into future building lots. Unfortunately the development standards of the day allowed the subdivision to occur with no utilities and little regard for what was actually on the ground. Scores of building lots looked feasible on paper but in reality were under water much of the year or on unstable soil. Some lots, though, had been platted on the former parade ground, centrally located and surrounded by some of the remaining historically interesting buildings. The only thing impeding development was the lack of utility services.

The old fort had been served by rudimentary sewer and water systems. The water system had been assumed by a local private water company, but sewers were another matter. A public sewer district was formed to operate and maintain the former fort's system serving the existing residential properties. But it was not capable of serving all the lots that had been created on paper. This circumstance served to effectively prevent development on the old parade ground for several decades as it slowly succumbed to blackberries and scrub brush.

Two things happened to alter this status quo: new environmental regulatory requirements meant that the sewer district would have to build a modern wastewater treatment plant, and the demand for residential property in our community suddenly made building lots that had already gone through a subdivision process *very* popular. Things were about to change and the open space in the heart of the neighborhood, albeit neglected, was threatened.

Even though it had been subdivided for many years, most of the site was under single ownership. When a row of houses was built facing an abutting street, the neighborhood was galvanized into action. They approached the developer who owned the bulk of the remaining lots with a proposal: Would he delay development or sale of the lots while the neighbors looked for a way to buy them all and preserve the open space and commemorate the historic parade ground? He agreed, but time was of the essence.

A handful of the lots remaining on the periphery had been sold over the years and the neighbors went to work contacting the owners to determine if they would participate in a plan to preserve the parade ground. A few chose not to, but ultimately a complicated plan evolved that involved the developer, two neighboring property owners, the city, and the countywide housing authority.

Here is what was arranged:

- One lot in the parade ground was owned by the residents of one of the historic buildings across the street. They offered to donate it.

- The city was asked to purchase two more individually owned lots in the parade ground in what was essentially a "two for the price of one" offer from the owner.

- The developer would sell his ownership to the housing authority.

- The city would authorize a revision of the subdivision allowing the housing authority to concentrate a new development of market rate and subsidized housing units in one corner of the property at less than the underlying density.

- The remainder of the property would become the Parade Ground Park.

In the end, by killing this "zombie subdivision," an important historical element of the community was preserved through the generosity, energy, and creativity of key neighbors, the city and housing authority staff, and a patient and cooperative developer.

Getting What You Want Through Foresight and Creativity: Part 5

Sometimes products or services that benefit your community come from unlikely sources. Who would have guessed that a defense contractor and a commercial fishing net manufacturer would have anything to offer a local government? I certainly didn't before I toured their respective facilities.

Silence Is Golden

As a city official you're often invited to meet local business owners to learn about their businesses, what they contribute to the economy, and how the city's rules and regulations either benefit or interfere with their ability to achieve a positive bottom line. For the most part these meetings provide interesting and enjoyable forays out of the office and they always improve your appreciation for the diversity of your local economy.

On one occasion I toured the offices of a small engineering company located on the edge of our central business district, assuming that they might be a potential resource for the city's typical civil engineering needs. I was surprised that the firm was not your typical civil engineering firm at all but actually an important defense contractor. Their area of expertise was acoustics.

Imagine a ship, and particularly a submarine, as a big metal container with lots of moving parts inside rattling around. Other ships—especially those belonging to folks who don't like you—spend a lot of time listening for those random sounds so they can find you and sink you if a shooting war breaks out. This little company contracted with the US Navy and specialized in tracking down the sounds of all the pumps, motors, and thousands of other moving parts on a ship that might be on the verge of breaking down. You know, the "squeaky wheel" in need of grease. Finding it those early not only saves money on unexpected and untimely breakdowns but also keeps it them quiet when you don't want to give the bad guys an easy target.

It quickly occurred to me that our city had many pumps and motors moving water and sewage from place to place. A breakdown anywhere in those systems would result in consequences ranging from annoying to catastrophic.

We asked the company if they'd ever done an analysis of a municipal utility system. Though they hadn't, they were interested. In a short while we had a thorough report on the condition of all our water and wastewater facilities. Their analysis revealed that one pump, deeply submerged in a critical sewer lift station, showed indications of an imminent breakdown. We ordered replacement parts and repaired the pump in an orderly fashion under non-emergency conditions. Had the pump failed while in service it would likely have resulted in untold overtime costs, disruption of sewer service to a portion of the city, and potential environmental damage from overflowing raw sewage. The public works director estimated that we probably saved much more than the cost of the analysis.

Cast Your Net Upon the . . . um, "Waters"

Another inspiration came following a tour of a firm that used a massive sophisticated knitting machine to construct nets for the deep-sea fishing industry. I learned much I hadn't known about commercial fishing as well as the nature of this particular business.

Later, the staff at the city's wastewater treatment plant reported a persistent problem with birds getting into the open primary and secondary clarifier tanks at the plant. I remembered the knitting machine. Maybe the company would make a circular net to cover those tanks. A call confirmed that the equipment could be programmed to create any size we might need. The built-in elasticity in the fabrication was perfect for our facilities. The business owners were pleased to supply a solution that met a need in their hometown, and the city got a solution to a pesky problem, through a creative adaptation of an unlikely product.

You never know where the solution to a problem will come from. Keep your eyes and ears open and your imagination active.

Assume Nothing—It's Probably Not as Good as It Seems

First Impressions

Whether you're newly elected or have just been appointed to a senior management position, you're inheriting an efficient and smoothly running organization. Each and every operation is well-documented, and procedures and policies have been adopted and implemented so that all employees understand their roles and perform their duties with expertise, courtesy, and efficiency. You can sleep well at night knowing that your agency is in good hands.

Yeah, right.

Even in the best organizations improvements may be needed. Some may have already been brought to your attention before your first day on the job. Or, it actually may appear that everything is running smoothly and efficiently. Either way, you and your staff will benefit by taking the time to systematically deal with whatever deficiencies exist in a way that will have lasting dividends for the organization, its employees, and the public.

Up-to-date procedures are valuable for employee performance review as well. Poor employee performance may be the result of good employees following outdated procedures.

Here are some methods to consider to improve the performance of your organization.

Don't Follow the "If It Ain't Broke, Don't Fix It" Rule

It's a clever catchphrase and can bring a chuckle when delivered in the right context. But don't use it as a guiding management principle.

Procedures that allow processes to run quite smoothly in the absence of any formal, documented policy can evolve in mature organizations. On the other hand, the procedures actually being followed may bear absolutely no resemblance to what may have been written down at some time in the past. When the system is put under stress—whether from rapid growth, a major annexation, or severe budget reductions such as those brought about by the recent economic recession—it is bound to fail. Making the assumption that "if it ain't broke, don't fix it" can present you with a nasty surprise.

Employees may have established a pattern of work flow in which they pass the product on to the next person without fully understanding the whole process and how their individual contribution fits in. Adding new people to the chain, physically moving them to another room or building, or removing one or more individuals can drastically upset a process that seemed to be working fine. Without a well-documented procedural policy in place that reflects what's actually being done and why, you and your staff won't know what's wrong until some key process breaks down.

For example, in one small city a major annexation resulted in several new positions being created in the finance department, which also supported the city's utilities. Some employees were reassigned and others relocated. After several months, a stack of unprocessed forms for creating new pages in the water meter reading books was discovered. Several new accounts had gone unbilled because the new pages hadn't been inserted in the meter reader's books. The person who took in the information had dutifully filled out the forms and put them in the usual place, but that's where they stopped due to the staff changes and physical rearrangement. The meter reader noticed occupied places that didn't seem to be in his books and went to the office to ask about the discrepancies. Only then did the people involved recognize that the system had broken down. Understanding what they were actually doing and having a written procedure, beyond just "Fill this out and put it here," would have avoided this near-miss of embarrassment and lost revenue.

Another characteristic of bureaucracies is that what may start out as a simple policy or procedure can accrete layers of complexity (somewhat like an onion) in response to various challenges or occurrences. Sometimes these are necessary adaptations to changes in the needs or demands of the citizenry, or changes in the regulatory, legal, or political environment. At other times, these added "workarounds" and steps in a process are simply responding to one-time events or anomalies. They become a permanent part of the process "in case it happens again." The added inefficiency far outweighs the need for the "just in case" step to be added to the process.

Whether evolution has been necessary or not, a thorough review can separate the necessary elements of the process from the superfluous and assure that what is being done is efficient and effective.

Analyze

Begin by making a thorough analysis of the process you want to review. Resist the temptation to conclude that you know what's wrong and impose an immediate fix. Often there are details that aren't readily apparent and need to be considered to avoid other unintended consequences from acting abruptly. On the other hand, you need to keep things running, so you may have to put on a Band-Aid until a more detailed diagnosis can reveal any systemic problems that need more in-depth attention.

Observe

The first step in your analysis should simply be to observe what's going on—who does what and what do they do? Spend enough time with the people doing the work so you can see what steps are involved in the tasks they do, who they interact with, and what they work with.

Question

Ask questions of the staff about their reporting relationships, what happens to their work product after they've finished with it, and what they understand about why they do it. This can be done in a casual, non-threatening way that demonstrates interest in the staff and their work environment, yet also yields the kind of candid insights you need to develop appropriate procedures. You may also need to conduct more structured interviews with key staff in the process you're examining in order to complete the picture.

Involve

Before you simply take all you've learned, draft a new policy, and tell everyone what to do, ask for input from those who will be responsible for carrying out the new policy. Present what you've learned from your observations and questions and ask if you've missed anything. People welcome the chance to offer suggestions for improvements. A valuable method that involves all the participants in the process under review is to break it down into individual steps, write them on small pieces of paper (Post-it® Notes are good for this), and stick them on the wall. Everyone can get involved here, since you want to make sure each discrete action is identified. Each note should represent only one step. Your wall becomes a giant flow chart. Bottlenecks, duplication of effort, and obstacles start to appear. Missing links become apparent and steps that add little or no value to the end product are also revealed. Depending on the size of the group, you can involve everyone to start streamlining the process, delegate it to a sub-group, or take it on yourself.

At this point, you've documented what you're doing and it's time to write it down in policy and procedure. There are many formats for this. The exact form or style of the written procedure is less important than making sure it represents what you need and what you want to be doing in direct and understandable language.

Change
When you're ready to institute the change in procedure, take time to fully inform the staff. Remind them of the help they provided in making it possible and empower them to speak up if they discover during the implementation process that it isn't working as intended. Adjust the procedure as needed, and be sure to revise the written documentation to reflect the adjustment.

Review
Finally, set up a periodic review to determine if further adjustments are needed. As circumstances change, people will naturally adapt the routine they follow in response. Before long, the actual tasks being performed will no longer conform to the policy and procedure you've established. (Remember the onion.) Regular review is essential in determining whether corrective action needs to be taken regarding staff performance, or whether the elements of the

work have changed so much that written procedures need revision once again.

Remember to stay vigilant. Don't assume everything is fine—it may not be as good as it seems.

Street Names: Where Policy and History Meet

Wherever you travel, street names can help you find your way, confuse you, and/or demonstrate a remarkable lack of imagination. Very often they also tell you a bit about the history of the community. The name may relate easily to the history in an obvious way or it may require some sleuthing to uncover the meaning behind the name. Having a logical policy on street naming (or renaming) can prevent mix-ups and provide some insight for future generations in your community to avoid losing the original meaning, especially if the name was intended as a tribute.

Here are a few examples.

Cole Street – The main business street in one city I worked for was Cole Street. The local merchants group was known as the "Cole Street Gang." As far back as anyone could remember (or cared) that was it. However, in researching the title on a potential property acquisition, our engineering staff discovered that it was originally platted as Coal Street. They did a little digging (no pun intended!) and discovered that

171

sometime in the early 20th century the local business community wanted to create a cleaner image for the downtown. A name associated with ashes and soot just wouldn't do, so "Coal" became "Cole." Not earth-shattering but interesting. Maybe it was one of the first achievements of the "Cole Street Gang."

An interesting side note: a tiny section of Cole Street with perhaps two or three houses had been cut off many years earlier by a state highway project. It was only accessible in a roundabout way from another street. People were often lost and confused trying to find it and the Fire Department requested that the name be changed to match the street it was now connected to. It seemed like a logical thing to do in the interest of public safety and convenience. "No, no, no!" the handful of residents complained. "We don't want that street name. The houses on that street were cheaply built for workers on the nearby flood control dam." That had been nearly 50 years before! A year or two later the city changed it with no further discussion.

Adams – Like many communities, our early settlers laid out the street grid and chose to honor national historical figures (or trees). So we had Jefferson, Washington, Adams,

Garfield, Harding, Monroe, etc. After World War Two the community built a hospital on a block bounded on the south side by Adams Street. One of the physicians who served the community for many years was Dr. Gordon Adams, who also had volunteered as the city's Health Officer for much of that time. When he died the City Council considered some way to honor him, perhaps by naming something after him. Voilà! What could be more appropriate than renaming the street next to the hospital after *Doctor* Adams instead of *President* Adams? It seemed like it was meant to be, but as time passes will anyone remember?

Hawk and Hunter – A large regional homebuilder was in the process of developing the first significant residential development in our city in some time. The houses would be a nice addition to the community and the approval process was going smoothly. So we were surprised when the local Veterans of Foreign Wars post suddenly announced that they objected to the approval because the city had a "policy" of naming any new streets after local service members killed in the line of duty. Apparently the idea had been discussed in the past but had never been officially adopted or followed. Now that the VFW had made a point of it, the Mayor and

City Council thought it was important to respect the memory of those who had died in service to our country.

While the developer's project manager was sympathetic, he was adamant that they weren't going to change the names that had been carefully chosen at considerable expense by their marketing consultant to reflect a northwest outdoor adventure theme centered on nearby Mt. Rainier. After all, he said, the policy hadn't been followed for years. Why start now in the middle of their process?

The VFW was equally adamant. I looked over the list they gave me. Two names struck me: Hawk and Hunter. Both could easily fit into the theme of the development as well as honor the men. I called the developer and the VFW and suggested a compromise. The developer would drop two names from its list and substitute these two. It wasn't everything each side wanted but the deadlock was broken. The project moved to completion.

Welfare – Shortly after the city I was serving annexed a large, formerly unincorporated territory, we received a petition from a group of property owners living in the new area on Welfare Avenue. They requested that the city change the name of their street. It was a fairly affluent community and they thought the street name reflected poorly on them. Like me, many of the city staff members were relatively new and unfamiliar with local history. Fortunately, an active historical society caught the issue when it appeared in the local newspaper and promptly informed us that the street was named for an early settler family named "Welfare." The petitioners accepted the historic significance of their street name and their request was withdrawn.

Island/Ihland – These two street names are in use where I live. They sound exactly the same phonetically. Fortunately the potential for public safety dispatch confusion has been minimized with the advent of enhanced 911 technology, but no doubt ordinary voice communication still has trouble.

Lessons Learned

Lesson Number One–If you adopt a policy, write it down and follow it. Potentially embarrassing disagreements like the one between the VFW and the developer can be avoided if the street naming policy has been formally adopted and codified. In the 15 years I had worked there no one had ever mentioned such a policy. It was probably rediscovered by the VFW while someone was reviewing old records but since the city had not codified it there was no way for the current staff or elected officials to know it existed. The MRSC website has a page devoted to "Street Name Policies" with examples of a few ordinances.

Lesson Number Two–Work with the community to document the history and rationale behind existing street names. A local historical society, Boy Scout troop, school classes, or a senior center can help with research in figuring out what is behind the ones that aren't obvious. The results can be inspiring, informative, and even humorous. As generations pass, businesses come and go, and events are forgotten, the reasons behind some names given can be lost or obscured. Yet they are still part of a community's legacy and worth remembering.

Trash Talkin'

Something interesting always seems to turn up in the trash. In a previous article (See "Monday, Monday") I discussed the pitfalls of implementing a new solid waste collection policy that had the greatest impact on a single section of the community. Sometimes you've got to recommend something that will affect all or nearly all your customers.

No Sticker Shock

Our city had a long-standing policy of collecting unlimited amounts of trash from our residential customers on a weekly basis. Born out of pride in a clean community and supported by cheap tipping fees at a nearby landfill, our highly motivated crews picked up everything, even implementing some ad hoc recycling (long before recycling became the norm) by installing bins under the truck's compacter for containers of used motor oil and car batteries.

Eventually this policy became unsustainable. The county increased the tipping fees in anticipation of its eventual closure. In addition, our crews realized that residents from outside the city were bringing their trash and yard waste into town and dropping it off with friends. We knew that changing the policy would be difficult. We would face objections from our customers to paying for added service and we didn't have a method of billing for the service. We wanted to have the billing details worked out before going to the City Council with the change in policy, especially if there would be significant costs involved with billing changes.

Researching billing methods of local municipal and private haulers, we found that the most common system was route books similar to those carried by meter readers, in which the driver would note any additional trash containers picked up. The extras were added to the billing. This system worked well but would entail some cost to set up and operate. One hauler sold cardboard tags that the homeowner bought in advance and attached to any extra trash. The crew removed the tags and took them back to the office for resale. No record-keeping or billing was required. We liked the system but didn't like the pile of soiled, mangled tags waiting for resale. We devised brightly colored stickers the customer would apply to any extra bags or cans. The sticker either got tossed into the truck with a trash bag or was simply scraped off.

We settled on a two-can limit and included an explanation of the pre-paid sticker system to the City Council. The new policy was approved with little or no opposition. We prepared a clear explanation of the new system to our customers and mailed a flyer to every home that included two pre-paid stickers at no charge. The new system took effect with no appreciable impact on billing, record-keeping, or collection costs.

Lessons

When proposing a new policy or process, work it through to the likely conclusion to look for flaws that could derail it.

Imitation may be the sincerest form of flattery, but also look for ways to improve on what others are doing. Your colleagues in other jurisdictions are happy to share their experiences and appreciate learning if you've made improvements on their ideas as well.

Dumpster© Diving

Several years before I arrived as City Administrator, the city had purchased its first rolling trash containers to service customers with larger volumes of solid waste.

Unbeknownst to me, in the implementation process for this new service, the previous City Administrator had negotiated the rates charged to a majority of commercial customers. They were based generally on the number of standard garbage cans they had, multiplied by the frequency of collection. The more containers put into service, the better price the city got for them with the added benefit of significantly improving the collection process and overall appearance of downtown alleys. Unfortunately, none of this was recorded anywhere or authorized by ordinance.

In the ensuing years, the utility billing clerks had approximated the rates for a single container with weekly collection and routinely quoted that rate to new customers who then were billed and paid accordingly. They extrapolated these rates to calculate additional containers or more frequent collection as well.

Enter the new City Administrator—me—and a requirement for a rate increase to support the solid waste utility. I found the rates for single-family collection in the city code. But when I asked for a copy of the most recent ordinance setting the rates for containers, I was told there wasn't one and that my predecessor had played "Let's Make a Deal" to get the program off the ground. Oh boy!

I knew approximately how much money was necessary to keep the utility solvent, so I thought it would be easy to apply a modest rate increase across the board. But when I got to the commercial accounts I was in for a big surprise. Comparing the rates of most of our older commercial accounts to the rates the staff had been using for new customers, I discovered drastic discrepancies. Applying the current rate quoted to new customers to one of our larger established accounts with one of the negotiated rates would have resulted in an increase of over 1000%! That was politically impossible, and we simply didn't need that much money. What we needed instead was a fair rate that supported the operation and *was legally adopted.*

First, I determined the impact of a consistent rate uniformly applied. I had no intention of recommending it since I knew the impact it would have on some customers as well as the fact that it would yield far more revenue than we needed. Then I calculated a much more modest rate structure that was consistent for *all* accounts.

Second, I got a list of all the accounts with negotiated rates and calculated their individual bills in three ways: what they had been paying, what they would have paid based on what we'd been quoting new customers, and their payment according to the newly proposed rate structure.

Finally, I made appointments with the owners of all the businesses that would be affected. I explained that in the course of preparing the rate increase proposal I had discovered that their current bill was significantly below what we were currently billing others for similar service. I showed them the numbers and then explained the "good news": With the new structure, their bills would not need to be nearly that high at all and showed them the new "lower" (though actually quite a bit higher) bill.

Every customer responded positively. Our largest customer, a commercial cabinet shop, found a way to recycle much of its waste, reducing the bill and our disposal costs in the process. Our crew appreciated it too. They detested the wood dust and the fact that the material wouldn't compress in the compacter trucks, requiring extra trips to the landfill.

We implemented the new rates by ordinance.

Lessons

To paraphrase Forrest Gump, "City Hall is like a box of chocolates. You never know what you're going to get." Policies and procedures are often unwritten. Hopefully you won't find something this glaring. Once you get the situation straightened out, commit it to writing.

Communicate and be candid but avoid blame. There's an old joke about blaming your predecessor but that's generally not a good idea. If you've discovered criminal wrongdoing, that's another matter. But in this instance, as glaring as it was, I was aware that my predecessor was not an experienced public sector manager and I didn't see anything other than his best efforts to get a new service started.

Communicate in-person if you can. It's respectful and also allows you the opportunity to gauge the reaction to your message. You'll have a much better sense of whether there will be opposition to what you're proposing and if so how strong it might be. Most likely you will gain a measure of respect and trust and diffuse opposition.

When One Budget Closes, Another One Opens (But Where's the Cash?)

You may be asked about the proper way to handle the uncertainty around prognosticating how much you expect to have at the end of one budget cycle and the beginning of another. This problem has been especially vexing for the last few years as mayors, city managers, and finance directors have been looking under the seat cushions for loose change to balance their budgets. While you're looking for every dime, so are your tax- and rate-payers. Unexplainable carryovers from year to year are fair game for criticism.

In bygone days, agencies could afford to let a department that had accumulated a surplus during the year carry over some of it for unexpected exigencies. No more. Not only is this unlikely due to the fiscal realities of the times but it is also poor public policy. Strictly speaking, one might even argue that it is illegal given the opening lines of RCW 36.40.200, RCW 35.33.151, and RCW 35A.33.150 that state "All appropriations in any current operating fund shall lapse at the end of each fiscal year." The statutes do allow for the reality that operations don't simply end with the new fiscal year by allowing exceptions for ongoing capital projects and providing a means to pay for things "in the pipeline," ordered but not delivered by year's end.

Trying to establish a responsible estimate of ending cash balance is not easy, especially in complex organizations, but it's essential. It requires candid, two-way communication between your finance and operations staffs so an honest presentation can be made to elected officials and the public. Because the statutes allow some latitude so that each agency can respond to its own circumstances rather than applying a hard and fast rule, the best approach is one as transparent and easily explained as you can make it. If you can't explain it clearly you need to reconsider your policy.

In today's fiscal climate, it's never too late nor too early to address this question. Your staff needs to know what the rules are from the beginning and understand how you will be dealing with year-end issues so two-way communication between finance and operations becomes routine and not just a once-a-year exercise.

The beginning of the year is also a good time to explain to elected officials that there will always be some variance between the estimates of ending cash balance and the actual beginning cash balance at the start of the following year because of the timing of vendor invoices, unexpected expenses near the year-end, or expected expenses that are not incurred. At budget time, unencumbered funds should be shown as early as possible since they are part of the revenue available for the next year. This is obviously more important if the amounts are significant, and less so if they fall within the plus or minus amounts that may be needed to finish the year. This is where a candid relationship with department directors and managers pays off so you can estimate as accurately as possible what they'll need to close out the year.

Presenting Potentially Adverse or Controversial Budget Recommendations

Forming Rational Recommendations

It may seem that this commentary reflects the obvious—the presentation of difficult or controversial recommendations is simply a matter of "common sense." In general that is true; however, while the careful presentation of information is not always a guarantee of successful implementation, it is worth the extra effort to fully work through your report in explaining the issues. Thereafter, if things go awry, you know you did everything within your power to form and present a rational recommendation.

If you are presenting a combination of cost-cutting and revenue increases, present the cost-cutting recommendations first. Emphasize that it is your philosophy and that when faced with a budget shortfall, the leading recommendations should always be: "Where can we save?" In other words, you are answering the question before it is asked: "Are we getting the most out of collected revenue before we ask for more?"

Acknowledge that in the public sector, it is often traditional to think in terms of increasing revenue first. Admit, however, that one drawback to this belief is that operating costs are presumed to be optimal. Explain that you want to avoid that assumption until all possibilities have been evaluated.

If you propose cuts, be sure to describe any potential consequences. You may be able to come up with a cutback that has no negative consequences but there will most likely be a downside that has to be recognized, such as the costs associated with deferred maintenance. If so, say so rather than assume that everyone will understand this. You avoid having a critic point it out later at your expense.

Refresh Memories...But Beware of Old Controversies!

When beginning a discussion of an issue with a long history, it is important to refresh people's memories about what has transpired. Consider developing a chronology of prior events or actions. Be careful, though. If at some point in the past there had been a controversy, do not get sidetracked rehashing it. It's a waste of time and risks obscuring your recommendations with previous biases. This is especially true if you are new to your position, and the controversy occurred under different management. Likewise, even if they were correct in their position on the issue (whatever it was), do not waste your "stock" by getting drawn into the arguments of a past debate. Your job now is to move forward. If necessary, just cover the most recent events or the latest request the Council requested from you.

A few choice phrases to set a discussion in motion might be "As previously discussed [or authorized] by the Council...," or "At the [date] Council meeting, Council instructed that staff [accomplish the following]..." The important thing is to *subtly*—but *directly*—remind everyone that they have participated in the process leading to the presentation you are about to make. This approach also serves to remind other listeners that the particular news or recommendation was requested. Whatever you advocate, it is still *your* recommendation. You are only reminding them that this directive was asked of you, thereby establishing the reason why this recommendation is now forthcoming.

Adding Perspective...
When discussing rate increases, it is also valuable to add perspective: What is the relative impact of the increase on a typical customer or ratepayer? If rates have not increased over an extended period, demonstrate how the recommended increase on average measures up to some other benchmark, such as the Consumer Price Index (CPI), or the price of

another familiar commodity. But, again, be careful! Depending on the commodity, try not to be "flippant" with the equivalent product. In other words, take your community into account; for instance, if your audience views fancy coffee drinks with disdain, use the price of a regular cup of coffee instead of a latté.

...And Humor
Another way to connect is to consider the use of humor, though you need to know when to use it. Humor is a good tension-diffuser, but it can backfire if your audience does not "get it" or if people's jobs are potentially in jeopardy.

Using Comparables
To support a recommended increase in taxes, rates or fees, you may also want to include a comparison of rates or rate increases of nearby local governments or districts. Some boards or Councils may actually insist upon comparisons, while others may say "so what?" Your assessment of their expectations could be the determining factor. It probably doesn't hurt to ask if the decision-makers would like some comparative information if you don't already know.

If you compare, choose the counterpart(s) cautiously. Make sure they really are comparable. Your agency may already utilize some generally accepted benchmarks. If so, employ them, but take nothing for granted. Briefly explain again why they have been selected for comparison.

If the City does not have previously agreed-upon comparables, and you or your staff choose several for this purpose, take the time to clarify the rationale behind the selection(s) for the Council's and public's benefit.

Restating the Obvious
Careful preparation of your presentation may not guarantee success but paying attention to details in advance can enhance your effectiveness and focus discussion.

Final Note
This also an effective way to present information to the media.

The Value of Knowing a Little About a Lot

The International City/County Management Association (ICMA) Voluntary Credentialing program requires participating managers to test themselves in a variety of management skills—"core competencies" deemed critical to successful public management. Regular continuing education, self-evaluation, and independent review are required to maintain the designation of Credentialed Manager. As a Credentialed Manager for over ten years now, I recognize the importance of cultivating and enhancing these attributes. But they're not everything.

Don't misunderstand. To be an effective public manager you must be skilled in a number of critical areas: finance, personnel, human relations, organizational development, labor relations—even law—but from experience I've found there is tremendous value in knowing a little about a wide variety of subjects that may seem far removed from our core competencies.

This type of knowledge has helped me relate to the diversity of the people in the community and in the workforce. In addition, I've often drawn on experiences and knowledge unrelated to immediate situations to amplify my management skills.

Defusing Tension

A labor relations consultant who once assisted me with collective bargaining negotiations was a retired US Navy admiral. On more than one occasion during particularly difficult negotiations he would defuse a tense situation by telling an amusing anecdote from his long career. Everyone in the room benefited from the relief the laughter brought and productive negotiations resumed.

Establishing Rapport

When I accepted my first appointment as a City Administrator in the state of Washington, I was routinely referred to as the "young Californian." I'd graduated from UCLA and began my public service career in a suburb of Los Angeles. However, I grew up in Alaska and had spent the better part of my life up to that time in the 49th state rather than the state of the 49ers. I quickly learned that beginning a presentation to a community group by stating "I was born in Alaska…" was an effective "icebreaker" (pun intended). I even discovered that a local fire district commissioner was also from my hometown, albeit thirty or forty years before me. Nevertheless it gave us something in common when the interests of the city and the fire district were at odds. I believe it contributed to the goodwill necessary to solve problems.

Not only was there the relative novelty of my Alaskan childhood, but I also discovered that many of my experiences there—such as doing farm chores during stays with a friend at his family's log cabin homestead—provided me with insights into farming and life experiences that benefitted me as City Administrator of a city surrounded by dairy and horse farms. Those activities also gave me first-hand familiarity with a way of life shared by people of previous generations which was valuable in understanding and relating to them.

Understanding Specialists and Specialized Issues

Public management invariably includes the oversight of construction projects ranging from buildings to roads to pipelines. Knowledge of the basic details of construction practices as well as the intended functions of the project itself is invaluable. It may sound counterintuitive but understanding the details can help you grasp the big picture (See "Saving the $12,000 Closet"). Understanding a little bit about construction and design helps you communicate with project engineers and architects as well as in day-to-day interaction with your staff.

Where Does the Knowledge Come From?

You never know when a little tidbit of information you collect will come in handy. Several years ago I was observing a paving project. The lead worker on the job and I began to talk about the project and about asphalt paving in general. I asked him about how the paving industry had changed during his career. He mentioned that as the price of oil had risen, the refineries had improved the process of extracting more products from the crude oil. In so doing, the residual (the part mixed with gravel to make asphaltic concrete paving material) had become less resilient. That made the pavement more brittle and with a subsequently shorter wearing life on the road. At the time it was merely an interesting factoid, but over time I saw evidence of it as our street infrastructure aged. More than once that information came in handy in a conversation with a citizen or elected official about the city's street maintenance and construction.

Countless other conversations with contractors, engineers, architects, and technicians have provided similar bits of insight and information that can be called upon when presenting complex subjects to elected officials and community members who may not be familiar with the subject matter.

While it helps to be inquisitive and observant about specific projects your agency may be involved in, you can also call upon your personal life experience, summer and after-school jobs, and hobbies.

Working a summer job in construction on an apartment complex damaged by an earthquake, I saw firsthand how the building and facilities had been affected. These observations— together with the undergraduate geology courses I'd taken—helped me many years later to quickly grasp important concepts in emergency management planning and seismic building codes for my community.

Throughout my career I've found that hobbies and interests outside of paid work experience bring opportunities for gaining knowledge beyond the "core competencies" we regard as essential to be a good public manager. Your memory can be like the "junk drawer" everyone seems to have at home that's full of bits, pieces, and gadgets that come in handy when they're called upon.

Speed Dating: It's Not Just for Your Social Life

My elder son recently recruited me to participate in a process to develop a new generation of civically involved young adults. My first assignment was a pretty straightforward presentation about local government in the state of Washington, condensing "Civics 101" into an hour (with time for Q&A). No easy task, but he told me it was well-received. Enough so that I was invited back for what the group had dubbed "speed mentoring."

Loosely based on the concept of "speed dating," our sessions consisted of a room full of inquiring minds shifting from table to table at predetermined intervals to hear from and question mentors from various public service, not-for-profit, and public interest organizations. In the brief time allotted, I gave a quick overview of the career opportunities in local government management and my thoughts on the best way to prepare for and enter the profession. It was a very creative way to provide an opportunity for people to make contact with people in fields they might want to pursue.

This novel experience inspired me to think of how the "speed dating" model could be adapted to other local government activities. Here are a few.

Orienting Newly Elected Officials
How about an afternoon following local elections when the recently elected commissioners or council members are rotated among department representatives for one-on-one conversations? Topics could include not only the current issues facing the department but also an exchange of sufficient personal information to scale the focus down from the levels of the campaign to a more human level.

Encouraging Professional Development
As suggested by my experience, this could be offered to people interested in a career in public service as a single "career day" event or a method of introducing a number of people to potential mentors. Based on the "speed mentoring" event, follow-up discussions could be arranged as appropriate.

Candidate Recruitment
Local agencies with positions open for an upcoming election could each have a table at a pre-filing event. Citizens interested in running for office could get information about

the agency, the current issues it is facing, and the expectations of the office.

Public Engagement

An agency could use such an event to offer the public an opportunity to meet its officials face-to-face and talk about issues at a personal level.

Volunteer Recruitment

Most communities have a large array of non-profit organizations contributing valuable services to civic life that need board members, volunteers, and donors to keep them active and functioning. Such an event could showcase the opportunities for service available to those who might have time, skills, and expertise to spare.

I'm sure even more ideas for using the speed-dating model can be envisioned. A city councilmember once said that disseminating public information was more like speaking to a parade than to an auditorium. Your audience is constantly changing. This model takes that concept of an ever-changing audience to give you the opportunity to communicate with a fairly large number of people, yet in a more personal way. Think of the possibilities.

It's not just for your social life any more.

Getting What You Want Through Foresight and Creativity: Part 6

This Old House Recycling

A development site included an existing old home. Rather than demolish it the developer offered the old house to a local non-profit group whose mission was to provide affordable housing in the face of rapidly rising real estate values in our community. The only condition was that the housing group had to remove the old house by a fixed deadline. A benefactor was willing to underwrite the relocation cost to a temporary site if one could be found ahead of the wrecking crew.

The executive director of the housing group contacted me to ask if the city might allow temporary storage of the house at the city's public works maintenance yard. This would give them time to find a permanent site and raise the money needed for a final move and set up. Our community generally favored the preservation of both affordable housing and examples of its older architecture so I was interested in offering any help the city could provide. We discussed the logistics of moving the house to the maintenance yard but I was concerned that the building might remain there for quite some time while the group raised the additional funds for a home site and moving the house a second time. If we could find a permanent site now the house would only need to be moved once and the donor they already had would have that cost covered. Also the house would be available as an affordable unit that much sooner and be subjected to less potential damage from two moves and general deterioration while in storage.

Considering various options, I remembered that the city had an abandoned well on a piece of property in a residential neighborhood. The property had been purchased for the well site decades earlier but the water quality had been unsatisfactory and the well had been recently sealed and capped. State law would not allow the use of a utility asset like the well property to be used for affordable housing but if the property were transferred to the city's general fund it could be made available for that purpose. First we confirmed that the property had actually been paid for with funds from the water utility. We then obtained an appraisal from a civic minded local appraiser so that I could present a recommendation to the city council. I described how the city's contribution to the project would be through a payment from the general fund to the water fund for the fair market value of the property. The proposal included a long term lease to the non-profit housing board in return for a token payment since this would now be a legitimate general government purpose.

The city council approved the package and within a short time the house had been relocated and rehabilitated with the help of many volunteers. Quite a few city employees even volunteered to help as a community service project.

The property was large enough to accommodate more than one residential unit and a few years later a second small cottage was saved and added to the first house making yet another affordable dwelling available and adding a sense of architectural history to their new neighborhood.

The Three Envelopes

Early in my career I heard the only actual city manager joke I can recall. It tells the story of a young assistant about to accept his first position as a city manager. He meets with the former manager and asks for some words of wisdom. His predecessor tells him not to worry; he's left three numbered envelopes in the desk drawer. "If you find yourself in trouble over some issue and don't know where to turn, open envelope number one" he says. "If it happens again, remember envelope number two and if you ever need it, envelope number three."

Sure enough, an issue arises after the honeymoon period with the city council that the young manager doesn't know how to handle. He's beside himself with worry and thinks he's going to lose his job. Then he remembers the envelopes. He opens number one and reads: "Blame your predecessor." At the next council meeting he reports that the whole mess is the fault of the previous city manager. The council agrees and everything goes forward smoothly. Years pass before the next crisis looms.

Again the manager thinks he's out of options and is starting to clean out his desk when he comes across the envelopes, now starting to yellow with age. Opening number two he reads, "Reorganize." At the next council meeting he announces a bold plan to revamp the organization to meet the crisis. "Brilliant!" exclaims the council and the manager's career is back on track.

The now-seasoned manager expertly faces every challenge public service can throw at him until one day a new crisis looms that seems insurmountable. He confidently digs out the last envelope with the faded number three on it and reads: "Prepare three envelopes."

I'd like to offer my own version of the three envelopes.

Envelope Number One

Don't blame anyone. Face the music. If a staff member has let you down and you've been called on the carpet by your boss or the city council, take it standing up. You only make yourself look small by blaming someone else, even your predecessor. I've witnessed people publicly blaming a clerk or subordinate when something's gone wrong and I believe it only made the supposed "leader" look bad. It's your duty to develop the organization to serve the community. If you've depended on someone and they've failed you, deal with it in private. Either they deserve your wrath and appropriate disposition (or not), but it's your job to deal with their performance and the performance of the organization. Obviously false malicious and slanderous accusations leveled at you demand a different response, but I'm not talking about those.

Envelope Number Two
Everyone has their own style and they often want to put their stamp on the organization. But in my opinion, reorganization usually consumes more energy and resources than it returns in benefits. I believe that it is far better to involve the people in the organization and let them have a significant say in determining what "fixes" are necessary. The people on the front lines usually know exactly what it will take to improve your processes, the ones they deal with every day serving your community. I've successfully applied this principle myself and I've had the satisfaction of reading author/consultant Ken Miller's confirmation of the success of such principles in his books, *We Don't Make Widgets* and *Extreme Government Makeover*.

Envelope Number Three
Ah, the irony of the punch line. What can I say? This has little to say about how you serve and more about how you take care of yourself and your family. When I began my career, employment agreements between the city and the manager were rare. Now they're commonplace. It's a quid pro quo—you're committing to the community and the community is reciprocating by reducing the personal trauma of a professional parting of the ways. The International City/County Management Association (ICMA) has just published new guidelines for communities and managers going through a recruitment process:

Recruitment Guidelines for Selecting a Local Government Administrator
http://icma.org/en/icma/career_network/career_resources/rec ruitment_guidelines_handbook

These guidelines are extremely helpful to candidates and elected officials.

This should really be "envelope number one." You deal with it first and then put it away for that (hopefully) far-off day when it might be needed.

Finally, even if there is only one city manager joke, keep a sense of humor. It will help you maintain perspective. Many years ago I was working closely with our city attorney to resolve a rather difficult issue. I gave him a greeting card that read: "Someday we'll look back on all this and ... Puke!" It summed up the situation perfectly.

Today's World and Yesterday's Challenges

While waiting in the buffet line at a retirement reception for a colleague, I overheard a conversation between a couple of younger members of the group discussing the latest challenges facing public administrators and the agencies they served. As they shared their experiences, I couldn't help but think back to my first years in public service and the burning issues of that time: open meetings, shoreline management, public records, public disclosure, and binding arbitration. I remembered the first Association of Washington Cities Conference I attended where the recently enacted public disclosure law was being hotly debated in a workshop for elected officials. One speaker predicted that it would be impossible to find qualified candidates for public office once the requirements of the law were fully implemented. Many flatly stated that they would refuse to disclose detailed information about their personal finances. In the subsequent decades, public disclosure has become an accepted part of running for public office. None of those dire predictions have come to pass.

To be sure, many issues I've cited remain and have become more complex. But for the most part they're now part of the background environment we accept as part of the responsibilities we assume with a career in public service.

As my younger colleagues continued their discussion of the new issues they faced, I concluded that as daunting as they seemed to us at that moment, with time they would become part of our everyday world like those issues of my early career.

A Little Ad Hoc Mentoring

I worked for several years in the private sector as a consultant for a firm that provided services to public sector clients. At one point I was manning the firm's booth in the exhibit hall for a conference of local government officials. I struck up a conversation with a young woman representing another consultant in the adjacent booth. She told me she had a Master of Public Administration degree from a large public university but that her faculty advisor had strongly encouraged her against public service. I was truly surprised that a member of the faculty of a public administration program would be discouraging students from entering public service. She told me he was a retired city manager!

We all have bad days (and sometimes longer) in our careers but whatever had soured this man on public service was now being passed on to potential future leaders. Who knows how many others had heeded his advice? I expressed my disappointment about the poor advice she'd been given by this "advisor" and encouraged her to reconsider.

During more than three decades of public service I have tried my best to undo the negative impression of public service portrayed to her and many others. We need bright young people to replace us and face today's challenges.

I'm proud of one young intern who spent some time in my office during his undergraduate years and subsequently served in Iraq as a United States Army officer. I hope he could call on some of the experiences he had in city hall to assist the Iraqis he advised.

Along the way we touch many lives and we can only hope that whatever examples we set are positive. It's one of the ways that we "pay it forward."

The Life Cycles of Boards

During a training session conducted by the manager of our county-wide department of emergency management, she asked each participant to state any volunteer affiliation to which they devoted time and energy outside of their primary employment. Nearly everyone had at least one.

Since then, I have reflected on my own public service career of over thirty years and the volunteer service organizations with which I have been involved. I noted some interesting themes common to the evolution of leadership of both public agencies and private nonprofits.

I believe the origins and evolution of these boards, whether volunteer or elected, share common patterns. Examining the relationship of the policymakers to the organization and how the policymaking body develops and matures may help managers understand and recognize the phases of that process. That helps anticipate their needs as a board and how that development process affects the ability of the organization to fulfill its mission.

A Sheltered Workshop

While I was serving a city in the greater Seattle area, our city council was approached by the board of directors of an agency that provided skill training and employment experience for developmentally disabled adults. The state had grant money available for buying and renovating facilities for such agencies, provided a local government sponsor would apply for and administer the grant. This nonprofit had been renting space in a large warehouse from a bank that had repossessed it and wanted a potential buyer. The agency saw an opportunity to stop paying rent and have a permanent home. The bank saw an opportunity to dispose of a liability. The city council was promised that no city funds would be needed. The match would come from money already raised and a discount the bank offered from the appraised value. The basic terms of the grant were easily satisfied. The city council agreed to apply for the grant, take title to the property, and lease it to the agency.

One term of the grant was that the city had to maintain the agency (or another providing the same services) for a minimum of 20 years or turn the property back to the state. Without going into the financial details, suffice it to say the agency eventually fell into financial difficulty. The city council asked me to join its board of directors to help stabilize it, reasoning that it was better to try that than recruit and establish a new tenant meeting the state's grant terms.

The board had been initially made up primarily of parents of many of the clients. Their motivation was the welfare, healthy development, and potential independence of their children. Their intentions were good, and they accomplished a great deal through the first several years of operation. Now it appeared to be well-established in what they saw as a permanent home. Eventually board membership began to turn over as founding members aged and were replaced. The type of commitment shared by board members with a personal stake in the organization was supplanted by new members who had to make business decisions detached from the direct connection to the workers/clients. Strain soon developed between longtime board members who viewed the work of the agency as a personal service to the clients, and new ones grappling with the realities of trying to close the gap between the subsidy provided by state and federal agencies and the income derived from contracted piece work.

Without the vision and dedication of the founders to the goal of training and potential self-sufficiency of their children, the agency wouldn't have existed. Yet without the evolution toward a more businesslike model, the agency risked failure.

A Habitat for Humanity Affiliate

A second example of organizational development involved the establishment of a Habitat for Humanity affiliate in the county where the city I served was located. Looking for a way to put my personal values to work, as well as all those episodes of "This Old House" I'd watched, I attended a meeting of the local board of Habitat for Humanity. They were in the process of preparing a charter application to the national organization for official recognition. Although what I really wanted to do was pound nails, I was invited to join the board. I accepted the invitation and jumped right in.

Once we received our charter, the really hard work began. As we expanded the board beyond the first few enthusiastic volunteers, we recognized the need for many different skills to form the committees necessary to raise funds and to recruit and prepare the future occupants for the responsibility of homeownership of the houses we intended to build.

As the board expanded, so did conflict. Everyone wanted the same thing: providing decent, affordable housing for people living in substandard conditions. With the variety of talents needed to meet the needs of the board, however, came a variety of interpersonal styles. New members, recruited for their business acumen, were impatient with many older members who were more motivated by altruistic goals. Success in meeting the real human needs required a strong business model that would show donors—who were vital to keep the projects affordable—that we were responsible and capable of achieving the goals we set. I knew everyone wanted to succeed in eliminating poverty housing, but there were board meetings when an outside observer might not have been so sure. Hard noses ran headlong into tender hearts. Feelings were hurt. Some members resigned. With perseverance, the organization moved through this phase and successfully built, and continues to build, many homes throughout the county.

The City

Community members wanting a greater say in the development decisions affecting the community made multiple attempts over many years to gain a measure of home rule through incorporation or annexation. Finally, by a very narrow margin, voters approved an annexation to the adjacent small city. The population increased nearly 850% overnight.

Under state law, the original city had a council of five members. With the increased population, the law required two additional councilmembers. Statutorily the council could have asked for applicants, reviewed them, and directly appointed the two additional members. Instead, they announced they would hold an advisory election and appoint the two candidates receiving the highest number of votes. About a dozen candidates filed. Not surprisingly, reflecting the close results of the annexation election, a leader of the "Home Rule" committee and the former co-chair of the "No City" committee were the top two vote-getters. The incumbent city council kept their promise and appointed both to the new seven member council. A clear majority of the new group had favored the annexation. In fact, it was essentially 6 to 1. However, even the newly-appointed member formerly from the "No City" camp acknowledged that the election was over. He believed it was his obligation to see that the new city did the best it could to keep the promises made during the campaign and create an efficient organization.

For the next eleven years, as issues and councilmembers came and went, the composition of the city council was largely drawn from a fairly large pool of citizens who had been involved in the home rule campaign. Throughout this time, even though there was turnover in the membership, a majority of the city council shared the experience of working toward home rule and getting the new city off and running.

With the passage of time and population growth, new members of the community became involved in the issues of the day and wanted a voice on the city council. Eventually, a majority of the city council was composed of individuals who did not share in the common experience of the home rule campaign. They had other concerns related to current issues important to them. A group that had been relatively collegial became more confrontational as the newcomers challenged holdover councilmembers and the staff. Trying to define roles and responsibilities and establish effective working relationships Consumed a lot of time, energy, and money. The collegial bond shared by the council for many years was not a prerequisite to effective local government. But once it was lost, much organizational energy was expended simply trying to figure out how to work together. There was nothing similar to the shared goal of establishing the new city that the councilmembers once had in common.

True Believers, New Blood, Conflict

Each of these examples shares a common pattern. Beginning with a foundation of shared values and a focus on a common goal—social, political, or economic—the people involved initially join together for that primary purpose. These are what one might call the true believers. They are the visionaries willing to start organizations and institutions in order to achieve a goal they believe in.

At some point, whether from outside influences or because the founding group recognizes a need for additional skills, new blood is injected. Even when the injection is intentional and desired, there is a reaction. The founders may feel threatened by the questions, challenges, and ideas offered by the newcomers. They may perceive that the new members do not share their commitment to the principles on which the organization was founded. They may feel that their contributions are not recognized or appreciated. The new members sense these reactions as resistance and can become frustrated. Each faction feels that their contributions aren't valued and original goals of the group that initially motivated its formation can fall victim to the conflict.

Recognizing that these stages can affect any organization allows the members of the board and the staff to anticipate them before change occurs and take measures to integrate the new members. This is especially important when several new members are added simultaneously or over a short period of time. Private, not-for-profit boards may be able to do this more deliberately than public agencies with elected boards. Elections may tend to emphasize differences rather than commonalities but, nevertheless, it is preferable to make a concerted effort rather than do nothing. It may be helpful for staff members to provide formal and informal orientation sessions and make as much background information available as possible.

Acknowledge that there will be a difference in the perspective of the continuing members versus the new members and talk about it. Concentrate on what they may already have in common and build on that. This should be recognized as more than just a "get-acquainted" exercise, as important as that may be. The purpose is not, as a former city councilmember complained, to "stand in a circle, hold hands, and sing Kum ba yah" at the end of the day. Focusing on the organization's reason(s) for existence and the skills the individuals bring to it can minimize the potential for trivializing this process.

Regardless of the tensions, misunderstandings, and conflicts that inevitably seem to accompany the life cycle of policymaking bodies, all the members share an underlying goal, even if they have vastly different visions of how to achieve it. If not, they wouldn't have joined in the first place. Keeping that goal first and foremost can help you through the rough patches.

Connected to the Community

A residency requirement for a city's senior appointed management position is common. It's also usually a state law for a city manager and often a local ordinance for the chief administrative officer in a mayor/council city. While the current economic climate has made it difficult for anyone appointed to a new position to comply, residency laws usually also permit an exemption for city managers. Local codes and policies can be adapted to suit the circumstances if need be.

Many successful professionals, especially in urban areas, have worked entire careers for multiple jurisdictions without ever uprooting their families. I chose to live within the jurisdictions I served. I believe it benefitted me in gaining a deeper understanding and appreciation of the community, building a support system for me and my family, and improving my ability to assess and address the needs of the city. Here are some of the activities that connected me to the community. Whether you live and work in the same place or commute, any or all of these connections can enrich your life and add depth to your professional development in unexpected ways.

Casual Observation

As a CAO, you must make time to observe how things work, whether it's the functioning of your staff at their daily tasks or the way traffic moves through town. Once you arrive at the office you're in demand and it's easy for people, phones, and emails to consume your time. Before you know it, it's time for the council meeting or community forum or other demands for your "after-hours" time and you've hardly left the office. When you live in the community you have the benefit of spending less time commuting and some of your casual observations can be made as you go about your personal life. An after-dinner walk with the family allows a slow and close-up inspection of the city's infrastructure—sidewalks, storm drains, crosswalks, park facilities and more. Similarly, a bike ride gives you the opportunity to observe pavement conditions that often can't be seen from a moving car, not to mention the hazards particular to the cyclist like catch basin grates, cracks/concrete pavement joints, narrow shoulders, street sweeping problems and low-hanging branches. It's a chance to see how things work (or don't work), for yourself while you're spending time with the family or getting in a little workout.

Service Clubs

Many city managers/administrators belong to international service organizations such as Rotary, Kiwanis, or Lions. I can only think of one instance where a colleague told me that he had not joined a service club, whether by choice or by council direction in order to avoid any potential appearance of fairness issues. Service club membership is a common and logical extension of career public service. You not only establish a network of contacts that is a good cross-section of the community quickly but also become a real person at city hall rather than just one of "them" to the members. It can be awkward when a club member disagrees with a policy decision, but it gives you an opportunity for personal communication in a forum where the rules of the organization dictate an additional degree of respect for each other beyond common courtesy.

Obviously service club membership isn't unique to whether or not you live in the community but participation in after-hours and weekend events is easier when you're close by. More importantly, it multiplies other community connections.

Church or Faith Community
Participation in a church or other faith community is certainly not a prerequisite to being an effective city manager. However, if you belong to such a group it is another part of the fabric of the community, multiplying your connections and creating more opportunities for communication with the people you serve. I once used the ICMA Code of Ethics as a handout to lead a discussion in an adult Sunday School class.

Family and Youth Activities
If you have children you will most likely be involved in school and extracurricular activities such as sports, music, or theater. As the son of a city manager myself I know how hard it can be to juggle competing schedules. In the long-ago days before computers, my mother kept a large desk-blotter-sized calendar on the kitchen door with everyone's activities and appointments. Even so, my dad had a hard time getting to many of the activities and events that involved me and my sister and brothers. During my career, I spoke up when the city council was trying to schedule conflicting upcoming events and in most instances they were able to respect my wishes. (Although there was that one memorable rock

concert I had to forgo for a budget hearing, but that's another story…)

Spouse/Partner Connections

The professional or personal activities of your partner yield yet another source of connections to the community. Occasionally you may even find yourself doing double duty. My wife served several years on the Board of Trustees for a community college in a neighboring city. On many occasions I accompanied her both as spouse and as representative of my city. I'm convinced that this connection in particular added to both the quality of life in our community and our personal quality of life. The connections I made with people from my community and the community college district through our involvement with the college added lifelong friendships as well as depth and richness to my experience.

Depending on the type of work their partner does, ICMA members need to be mindful of potential conflicts with the ICMA Code of Ethics. You don't want the potential benefits to your career to be ruined by an ethics violation. This caveat holds true for virtually all community involvements but that shouldn't prevent you from being involved in things beyond the office walls.

Non-profit Boards

You may have the pleasure and responsibility to be invited or volunteer to serve on the governing board of a non-profit organization. Like the examples I've discussed, you gain additional ties into the fabric of the community and at the same time the nonprofit benefits from your expertise and perspective. During my career I was privileged to serve on the boards of at least three widely varied organizations that served my community in ways beyond what the city could do. I gained insight into what they did for our town and I was able to assist them with management advice, policy development, and many other skills we exercise daily for the good of their organizations.

Incidental Connections

Contrary to the axiom "No good deed goes unpunished," sometimes a good deed comes back in a surprising way. My wife worked for a few years as the activity director for an assisted living center. One year for Veterans Day she asked if I could help her decorate the dining room for dinner. Since quite a few of the residents were World War Two veterans, I brought along a few model airplanes I'd built and collected over the years to use as decorations. Unbeknownst to me, one of the residents was the father of one of our public works department crew chiefs. He thanked me and told me how much it had meant to his father. During collective bargaining negotiations the following year, that same crew chief was on the employee team. While we may have disagreed on issues, I believe we both had a deeper level of respect and trust in each other as a result of that incidental connection that paid off in an improved collective bargaining process.

In another situation, a friend was the music director for a production of *My Fair Lady* at our community theater. Knowing I'd sung in a church choir, she asked me to help fill out the male voices in the chorus. Before I knew it I was singing and dancing in the Cockney quartet backing up Eliza Doolittle's "Wouldn't It Be Loverly." I even had a solo line and later in the show a speaking line in another role. I was so far outside my comfort zone that I wasn't uncomfortable anymore. A columnist for the local newspaper, extolling the virtues of community theater, said that in addition to the entertainment value you got to see the stage filled with local people of all ages and walks of life—even the city administrator. The city council was very understanding. I think I only missed one council meeting and one rehearsal.

Lynn Nordby

The Unofficial Role of the City Administrator

Seeking the benefits of professional management without the requirement of going through a formal election to change the form of government, many communities have chosen to create a position similar to that of a city manager under the authority of the mayor. The resulting hybrid form of government is often described as being "the best of both worlds" by combining elected leadership with professional management of day-to-day local operations.

Having worked in such a position for nearly my entire professional career in local government, I can answer the question "Is it truly the best of both worlds?" without the slightest sense of irony or hesitation: "yes and no."

The titles of city administrator and county administrator are commonly used, although chief administrative officer, supervisor, chief of staff, and, occasionally, deputy mayor are also applied. Numerous articles clearly articulate the textbook distinctions between the council-manager and mayor-council forms of government. But in practice personal and systemic characteristics intertwine in such a way that a simple factual comparison of the forms of government misses the subtleties of the unofficial role often played by the administrator in this hybrid form.

Under the mayor-council form of government, as defined by statute for most cities I'm familiar with in the state of Washington, all city staff members work for the mayor. Even staff members in positions described as responding solely to council needs are legally appointed by, and serve at the pleasure of, the mayor.

Administrator's Role
A pivotal but unofficial role of the administrator is to serve as a link between the mayor and the council. Clearly, a new administrator entering this arena should understand this and work quickly to establish credibility with the councilmembers. Usually, though not always, the establishment of the city administrator position is agreed upon by the mayor and council. That's a head start.

First and foremost, however, the mayor must have trust and confidence in the administrator. The Revised Code of Washington State that deals with cities operating under the "Optional Municipal Code" states:

RCW 35A.12.100

Duties and authority of the mayor:

The mayor shall be the chief executive and administrative officer of the city, in charge of all departments and employees, with authority to designate assistants and department heads. The mayor may appoint and remove a chief administrative officer or assistant administrative officer, if so provided by ordinance or charter. [Emphasis added.]

Any authority the administrator possesses comes from the mayor. As the statute states, the administrator is appointed by and serves at the pleasure of the mayor. At the same time, the administrator's relationship with the council is a key to effectiveness.

The administrator works for the mayor but must also work with the council. As the chief operating officer of the municipal corporation, the administrator must enjoy a high degree of confidence from the council. When the relationship between the mayor and council is strained, the administrator is legally aligned with the mayor.

If a relationship has been built with the council, however, the administrator may be able to function like a mediator. Though this can be extremely effective, it is also unofficial and involves a degree of risk. The administrator must be sensitive to just how closely either the mayor or the council can be drawn together. At the end of the day, the administrator still reports to the mayor.

Every mayor differs in personality, work style, communication style, and time commitments. The administrator must adapt to the unique characteristics of the mayor in order to work effectively for that individual and apply professional skills to the task of managing the city's operations.

Personal Experience

In some cases, the mayor might have outside employment or other interests that preclude being readily available for consultation. In such instances, the administrator sometimes can exercise considerable discretion and authority. To paraphrase a mayor I once worked closely with: "You take care of city hall, and I'll take care of my factory. Keep me informed; no surprises."

We worked as a team on those terms for nearly eight years. His "office" was a wire in-basket and a folding chair at the corner of my desk. In contrast, the next elected mayor had recently sold his business and was able to devote considerable time to the office.

He moved into an available office and spent many hours meeting with staff and citizens at city hall. The administrator can't take such a relationship for granted. As these contrasting examples illustrate, after the next election an entirely new working arrangement might be required; thus, perception and adaptability are crucial.

Legally, the mayor is the chief executive but ostensibly the office is a part-time job in many local governments. The mayor's presence may not be required all day, every day, particularly if they have chosen to delegate authority to the administrator for many daily details.

In other instances, regardless of the official status of the office, the mayor may be available for as many hours as the individual wishes to commit and can offer advice or give direction at any time. This can be advantageous when the mayor and the administrator work in sync and complement each other's skills and style in an agreed division of labor.

Confusion and conflict can occur, too. Sometimes, a mayor will make a management decision against the advice or in the absence of the administrator, with effects ranging from inconsequential to calamitous. The best relationship is one in which each trusts the other to support the other.

Ideally, the mayor needs to know the administrator will honestly, professionally, and effectively represent the mayor's position and decisions; in return, if the administrator says something—whether to a citizen, councilmember, or staff member—the administrator needs assurance that the mayor will support that.

Good and Bad

When this system works, it can be highly effective. When it doesn't, look out, because the mayor and the administrator can end up working at cross purposes. No mayor can be expected to accept that for long, if at all. If the working relationship can't be resolved, the mayor will usually end it.

The relationship with the council is legally predicated on the separation-of-powers concept wherein the council functions as the legislative branch and the mayor as the executive. In Washington State law, this is clearly spelled out in the council-manager statutes. Councilmembers are expressly prohibited from interfering in the manager's day-to-day administration of the city.

No such express prohibition exists in the mayor-council statutes. The mayor may assume a collegial role with the council or prefer to establish more of a bright line between policy and administration. Sometimes, the same mayor may operate in both spheres depending on the issue or perhaps in response to a change in the makeup of the council. The administrator is obliged to discern the subtleties of these shifts and respond appropriately.

Legally, as a mayoral appointee, the administrator is not answerable to the council. In practice, effective management by the administrator is impossible without a working relationship with the council. While the council cannot legally give the administrator directions, the administrator must walk a fine line between the clear executive authority of the mayor and the policy direction of the council. (Note that there is a difference between an administrator and a chief of staff, a position that exists in some larger cities. A chief of staff is often closely aligned politically with the mayor and leaves office at the end of the mayor's term; a typical administrator works apolitically through election cycles and may serve a series of mayors.)

Consequently, the administrator's relationship with the council, though unofficial, is invaluable. An administrator can't afford to deliberately alienate the council even though the administrator does not officially report to councilmembers. Having the confidence of the council proved invaluable to me at least twice during my career.

In one instance, the mayor died during his term. In another city, the mayor had to resign for a health-related reason. In both cases, the council's confidence in me permitted me to continue to manage the city and assist the council in the process of filling the vacancy in the mayor's office. Effectively, I was shifted into the role of city manager during the interim, then back again after the new mayor took office.

When the mayor and council are at odds, it sometimes takes tremendous time and effort on the part of the administrator to help the two parties find middle ground and make progress. Sometimes it can't be done. In that situation, assuming the administrator continues to enjoy the support of the mayor, they may find it extremely difficult to have recommendations acted upon favorably by the council.

Even if the administrator has been able to maintain a positive relationship with the council, councilmembers may take contrary positions because of antipathy toward the mayor. Conversely, success with the council on the part of the administrator may be perceived by the mayor as somehow a breach of the mayor-administrator relationship. Either way the administrator's effectiveness can be severely compromised.

On a positive note: in more than 30 years of my local government service—mostly in cities with the mayor-council form of government—the relationships were positive, productive, and collegial the vast majority of the time. Regardless of the legal distinctions in the form of government as defined by statute, the elected official's dedication to the good of the community brought the two positions together. When strains in relationships occurred, more often than not I was able to help find areas of agreement to build upon.

My father became a city manager in the latter half of his career, serving in Alaska, California, Oregon, and Montana.

As a city manager, the line of authority was clear for him: he was responsible to the city council. We had many opportunities to compare notes on our experiences, and more than once he said, "Son, I don't know how you do it!"

So, after 30 years of experience serving in positions as an administrator in mayor-council communities, was it the best of both worlds? My answer remains: yes and no!

This article first appeared in the ICMA publication, Public Management. Used with permission.

Is Leadership Overrated?

I had the privilege to attend the 2015 ICMA Gettysburg Leadership Institute, *In the Footsteps of Leaders*, a few weeks ago. Indeed, that pivotal three day engagement in July 1863 between the Confederate Army of Northern Virginia led by General Robert E. Lee and the Union Army of the Potomac led by General George Meade, provides innumerable examples of leadership, good and bad, exhibited by the officers and men of both armies.

Veritable libraries full of books have been written about the leadership skills exhibited by the men now immortalized in bronze on the former battlefield. So much so, that I found it difficult to express my own thoughts on the leadership lessons learned. In following up on our discussions during the Institute, I discovered a rarely considered perspective on leadership that gives a new dimension to these men.

They were followers as well as leaders.

In a recent Officer.com article about leadership, Edward Pallas and Al Uy describe Union cavalry General John Buford's exemplary "followership". They assert that his attributes as a follower were what inspired him to go beyond the typical role of the cavalry, which was simply to reconnoiter and report. At Gettysburg, Buford ordered his troops to dismount, assume the role of infantry (giving the impression of a much larger force), and take and hold a strategically strong position against a larger approaching Confederate force, thereby buying valuable time for the bulk of the Union army to arrive.

Followership isn't the antithesis of leadership, rather, a good follower is a collaborator in the success of organizational goals. Pallas and Uy cite Robert Kelly, author and organizational development consultant, and write that an exemplary follower must be:

"...an independent, critical thinker and be actively engaged in the organization. Critical thinkers are their own person and think for themselves. They give constructive criticism and are innovative and creative. When defining active engagement Kelly states the best followers take initiative, take ownership of the situation, are committed to the goals of the organization, and go above and beyond the job."

This certainly describes the initiative shown by General Buford at Gettysburg.

In Kelly's 1992 book, The Power of Followership, he observed that most people, no matter how impressive their rank or title, spend more time as followers than as leaders.

He suggests more time is spent reporting to people rather than having people report to us.

In a typical organization one expects that there are more followers than leaders, yet when have you heard about a "Followership Training Program"? I suspect if you did, you would think it was a joke. As business consultants and authors Don Grayson & Ryan Speckhart observe:

"...little effort is expended to train effective followers. For every follower training program, there are thousands of leader training programs. This disparity exists despite the fact that there are significantly more followers than leaders, particularly when you consider that all leaders are also followers. Even the CEO reporting to a board of directors is a follower..."

Grayson and Speckhart make five observations on the leader-follower relationship based on years of experience in consulting psychology with organizations.

1. **Leadership is "overvalued".** Not everyone is suited to be a leader and too much emphasis on developing leadership skills in everyone is wasteful. This is why a majority of employees don't have confidence in their leaders. Foster leadership in those with the right qualities, but don't fail to invest in the bulk of the followers as well.

2. **Developing better followership skills is vital and more valuable.** All of the current trends are toward flatter, less hierarchical organizations. Combine this with technological advances that are leveling the playing field as well and is the result is less informational disparity between leaders and followers than ever before. Often the follower contributes directly to organizational success through first person contact with clients and customers. They are very often the most visible representatives of your brand to the rest of the world.

3. **Being "number two" is a legitimate position and should be considered a career option.** People are often intimidated by "the boss". Perhaps not intentionally, but experience shows that the higher a person goes up the organizational pyramid the less candid feedback they receive. An effective "number two" can be the one to provide analysis, state contrary opinions, speak for others, and make recommendations to the leader when others might not be as likely to.

Rather than consider such a position as second rate or not quite "ready for prime time," the number two should be recognized as a valuable asset.

4. **Successful leaders and followers collaborate.** There are points at which the distinctions become clearer, but the

overwhelming emphasis on leadership development and the cult-like reverence for high profile charismatic leaders has skewed the perception that leadership is everything. It's not.

The authors suggest that in the early stages of a project the leader defines the scope, goals, and limitations, but as the project progresses, collaboration begins as followers step up and offer ideas, opinions and critiques. Finally, as the project nears completion, the roles become more defined as the leader defines the end of the project. Optimally the culmination would be a collaborative "lessons learned" wrap up.

5. **Followership has no following.** Unlike leadership with a wealth of material available to guide training, there is a dearth of followership training aids. It is just as important for leaders to seek ways to develop effective followers as it is to work on their own leadership skills.

According to Barbara Kellerman, lecturer at Harvard's John F. Kennedy School of Government and author of *Followership: How Followers are Creating Change and Changing Leaders,* the leveling of the playing field described by Grayson and Speckhart has changed the notion that leaders lead and followers follow, giving followers more power. Good leadership comes from learning to be a good follower.

Kellerman highlights five skills learned from being a good follower that will make you a better leader.

1. **Awareness**– Understanding and appreciating the needs of others is critical. A leader that is "tuned in," whether it be to customers, employees, colleagues, or board members, knows what motivates or demotivates them.

2. **Diplomacy** – Followers know when getting along is the right thing to do. Not every battle is worth fighting. A diplomat can work with someone with differences while not ignoring those differences.

3. **Courage** - A good follower has the courage to dissent when a leader, manager, or superior, is headed off track, Kellerman says. The same traits of a good leader guts and strength of conviction, are essential.

4. **Collaboration** – Kellerman echoes Grayson and Speckhart's observation that collaboration is an essential aspect of followership that leaders need to embrace. The CEO is rarely the only one responsible for the latest product or innovation. More often than not there is a team involved. Collaborative, aware, and diplomatic leaders who understand the followership role share credit when credit is due.

5. Critical Thinking - In order to be a good follower, you need to be able to think for yourself says *Ronald E. Riggio, Ph.D., associate dean of the faculty at the Kravis Leadership Institute at Claremont McKenna College in Claremont, California.*, "Many of the same qualities that we admire in leaders—competence, motivation, intelligence—are the same qualities that we want in the very best followers. Moreover, leaders, regardless of their level, also need to follow."

This brings us back to General Buford. He didn't just do what was expected of him as a cavalry officer. His understanding of the overall mission, critical thinking, and innovation as an outstanding *follower* made him the first of many pivotal *leaders* on those three fateful days in July 1863 that marked a major turning point in the struggle to preserve the United States.

Making a Difference

I've always held the opinion that most of my colleagues in public management and most public employees are generally motivated by a call to service. To borrow from an old U.S. Army recruiting slogan, "It's not just a job…" It's gratifying to see this opinion substantiated by academia. Jim Perry of Indiana University, for example, calls it "public-service motivation."

In his book *Extreme Government Makeover* Ken Miller observes that the majority of public employees are motivated by a desire to make a difference. In the February 2013 issue of *Bob Behn's Performance Leadership Report*, Behn cites new research by McKinsey and Company in their January 2013 *McKinsey Quarterly* describing a so-called Meaning Quotient (MQ) that they believe all employees want from their toils. McKinsey's report is about private sector workers but Behn says:

> For public-sector employees, McKinsey's "Meaning Quotient" is inherently large. It might be protecting vulnerable children. It might be creating the infrastructure that facilitates better economic

development and more employment. It might be ensuring that marketplace for financial securities, or for housing, or for employment is fair for all. It might be defending the country.

McKinsey describes the motivational benefit from "small unexpected rewards." Though the public sector can't offer the kind of perks afforded private-sector employees, Behn suggests that "public executives can employ a variety of intrinsic rewards and esteem opportunities to demonstrate that the accomplishments of individuals and teams are appreciated."

Showing genuine appreciation to your staff is effective in any organization and will pay dividends. Behn takes this message beyond just the employees, adding that "Still, it would certainly help if public executives told a few stories to remind employees, citizens, and potential employees of the meaning involved in all of government work."

This is a responsibility of public sector leaders and managers. Negative stereotypes are all too easy to accept and it's equally easy to take good work for granted. Make the time for positive reinforcement and for acknowledging accomplishments publicly. While it is important to recognize a whistleblower for exposing waste or wrongdoing, it isn't just an exercise in PR to give recognition for good work— it's leadership and good management.

I hope that you've enjoyed reading some of my stories and that perhaps they've encouraged you and reinforced your choice of a public service career for its "meaning quotient."

About the Author

Lynn Karl Nordby has over 30 years of local government management experience. Since 2008 he has been a public policy and management consultant with MRSC, a private non-profit based in Seattle, Washington dedicated to state-wide local government excellence through collaborative consultation and immediate access to a vast research and knowledge base. He currently serves as the Secretary-Treasurer of the Washington City/County Management Association. He holds a Master of Public Administration degree and is a Credentialed Manager through the ICMA voluntary credentialing program.

Mr. Nordby has three adult children and lives in the Seattle area with his wife Benay, author and homemaker.

CPSIA information can be obtained
at www.ICGtesting.com
Printed in the USA
FSOW01n0202150316
17892FS

9 781634 912426